CONTEMPORARY
AMERICAN
POETRY

*Studies in
Language and
Literature*

CONTEMPORARY AMERICAN POETRY

BY

RALPH J. MILLS, JR.

UNIVERSITY OF ILLINOIS AT CHICAGO CIRCLE

Random House
New York

*Acknowledgments are gratefully extended to the following authors,
publishers, and agents for their kind permission to quote from copy-
righted poetry.*

Brother Antoninus (William Everson) for excerpts from *The Masculine Dead*, The Press of James A. Decker, Prairie City, Illinois,
1942.
City Lights Books for "Laying the Dust," "Something to Wear,"
"The Marriage, II" from Denise Levertov: *Here and Now.* Copyright © 1957 by Denise Levertov.
Cresset Press, Ltd. for an excerpt from Denise Levertov [Levertoff]:
The Double Image.
Doubleday and Company, Inc., for "Sleep-tossed I Lie," Copyright
© 1962 by Brother Antoninus, "I Am Long Weaned," Copyright
© 1962 by The Poetry Seminar, Inc., from the book *The Hazards
of Holiness* by Brother Antoninus; to Doubleday and Company,
Inc., and to Beatrice Roethke for "Transplanting" and excerpts
from *Words for the Wind* by Theodore Roethke, Copyright ©
1958 by Theodore Roethke; to Doubleday and Company, Inc., for
an excerpt from "The Long Waters," from the book *The Far Field*
by Theodore Roethke, Copyright © 1962 by Beatrice Roethke, as
Administratrix of the Estate of Theodore Roethke.
Harcourt, Brace & World, Inc., and Faber and Faber, Ltd.: for

1912, 1916, 1918, 1919, 1924, 1928, 1931, 1933, 1934, 1935, 1940, 1944, 1945, 1946, 1950 by The Macmillan Company.

New Directions, Inc., for "Between Walls" from *Collected Earlier Poems*, by William Carlos Williams. For "With Eyes at the Back of Our Heads" and excerpts from *With Eyes at the Back of Our Heads*, by Denise Levertov, Copyright 1958, 1959 by Denise Levertov Goodman. For excerpts from *The Jacob's Ladder*, by Denise Levertov, Copyright 1958, 1959, 1960, 1961 by Denise Levertov Goodman. For "Winter Plowing" and excerpts from *The Residual Years*, by William Everson, Copyright 1948 by New Directions.

Oxford University Press, Inc., and Chatto & Windus, Ltd., for quotations from *Collected Poems 1930-1960*, by Richard Eberhart, © 1960 by Richard Eberhart. For an excerpt from *Undercliff: Poems 1946-1953*, by Richard Eberhart, Copyright 1953 by Richard Eberhart.

Random House, Inc., for excerpts from the following books by Karl Shapiro: *Trial of a Poet*, Copyright 1947 by Karl Shapiro; *Poems 1940-1953*, Copyright 1940, 1941, 1942, 1943, 1944, 1945, 1946, 1947, 1948, 1949, 1950, 1951, 1952, 1953 by Karl Shapiro; *The Bourgeois Poet*, Copyright 1962, 1963, 1964 by Karl Shapiro.

The University of Chicago Press for an excerpt from *Mallarmé*, by Wallace Fowlie. For "On Looking in the Looking Glass" and excerpts from *The Looking Glass*, by Isabella Gardner, Copyright 1961 by the University of Chicago.

The University of Detroit Press for excerpts from *The Crooked Lines of God*, by Brother Antoninus.

The University of North Carolina Press for an excerpt from "Devils and Angels" in *Collected Verse Plays*, by Richard Eberhart.

Wesleyan University Press for "Saint Judas," Copyright 1956 by James Wright; excerpts from "The Morality of Poetry," Copyright 1957 by James Wright; excerpts from "At the Executed Murderer's Grave," Copyright 1958 by James Wright, reprinted from *Saint Judas*, by James Wright. For "A Blessing," Copyright 1961 by James Wright; "Fear Is What Quickens Me," Copyright 1961 by James Wright; "Eisenhower's Visit to Franco," Copyright 1962 by James Wright; "A Dream of Burial," Copyright 1962 by James Wright, reprinted from *The Branch Will Not Break*, by James Wright.

Yale University Press for "A Girl in a Window" and excerpts from *The Green Wall*, by James Wright.

In Memory of My Father

"Friend and dear friend and a planet's encouragement . . ."
WALLACE STEVENS

Foreword

Many poets who certainly belong in these pages have been omitted for reasons of space. If I listed all I should have liked to include, the number would be disconcerting. A rather lengthy bibliography at the back of the book names most of those I have left out of the text. This bibliography should help the interested reader to sample the poetry of these years or to read thoroughly if he chooses. The studies themselves were not planned as exhaustive exegeses or as definitive interpretations, but rather as interpretive essays which will, I hope, encourage the student or general reader to become acquainted with contemporary American poetry for himself.

Some of these studies or portions thereof have appeared elsewhere in different form. The author wishes to thank the editors of *Chicago Review, The Christian Scholar, Modern Age,* and *Northwestern University Tri-Quarterly* for permission to use material which originally appeared in their pages. Thanks are also due the Northwestern University Press for permission to use here a revised version of my chapter on Theodore Roethke from *Poets in Progress,* edited by Edward B. Hungerford. I am grateful to Geoffrey Hartman, Richard Eberhart, Brother Antoninus, James E. Miller, Jr., Mark Perlberg, Nathan A. Scott, Jr., and to my editor David Dushkin for various kinds of help and encouragement. I wish finally to thank Mrs. Wells Chamberlin for her typing of the manuscript of this book.

RALPH J. MILLS, JR.

Department of English
University of Illinois at Chicago Circle

Contents

CONTEMPORARY
AMERICAN
POETRY

Introduction

In treating the poetry written in English from about 1910 onwards it has become more and more necessary in recent years to draw lines helpful in locating differences in generation, attitude, and endeavor among the authors of that poetry. It is also important to introduce readers to poets whose work and careers have appeared later than or to one side of the major movements or groups that sprang up so readily in the general atmosphere of artistic experimentation extending through the two decades from 1910 to 1930. That "modernist" or "post-Symbolist" revolution was, of course, a widespread aesthetic phenomenon not restricted to one or two countries or to poetry alone. The overthrow of existing literary conventions for the sake of a vision in closer correspondence with the radically changing realities of modern life paralleled similar departures from the past in painting, sculpture, architecture, music, and the dance. R. P. Blackmur, in his *Anni Mirabiles 1921-1925*, gives another name, "expressionism," to the significant literature produced with such astonishing genius and variety during the period of this revolution and finds in it the dual intention of embodying the actuality of modern existence and, simultaneously, of probing that actuality morally and spiritually by means of new and singular imaginative techniques. Blackmur writes:

> In expressionistic art we see what the forces are which we have to control by other means: the actual forces of human nature, of nonrational behavior, and

of the industriously rational machinations of the devil—the diabolic, the daemonic, and the chthonic —the life that is in our soil. Expressionism compacts the Faustian spirit and the adventures of our conduct. This is a new claim for the arts, and perhaps the most ambitious yet in the long series since Aristotle. It is precisely the opposite from Shelley's claim that poets are the unacknowledged legislators of the world. It constitutes for itself rather the claim to undermine, to readjust, to put into fresh order the frames or forms in which we make the adventure of conduct tangible to our minds, and it therefore denies validity to pre-existent legislation on human relations.

If we accept this complex passage as descriptive of the concerted effort behind the writings of Eliot, Yeats, Lawrence, Pound, Joyce, Mann, Benn, Rilke, Apollinaire, and many others, then we must also recognize that as a fabulous literary movement—erupting from a mixture of causes external to art which we cannot fully explain but will refer to here as social unrest, a world war, the miraculously rapid development of science and technology, and the discoveries of psychoanalysis—it was bound to win certain victories, and, at last, gradually to lose its creative momentum. The decade of the 1930s brought new political and social dilemmas, and in a short time the world was plunged again into disastrous conflict.

America contributed two (Eliot and Pound) and Ireland one (Yeats) of the three major revolutionary poets who established the "modernist" movement in English and American verse. Eliot and Pound began to lay down as well the critical principles that would eventually enable the revolutionary doctrine to become the norm rather than the exception. We are quite familiar with the outcome of that story these days: how Eliot and Pound did away with Victorian and Georgian poetic modes, introduced symbolism, irony, dramatic devices, conversational diction and the rhythms of modern speech; and how they faced squarely in their art the qualities of a fast-moving and tragic age. Though they were hardly the sole poets in the English language to perform in this way, they were the influential pioneers. Aided by I. A. Richards, and later by William Empson, F. R. Leavis, Cleanth Brooks, Allen Tate, and other critics, these poets effected a revolution in criticism and poetic theory that finally made them arbiters of literary taste and judgment. Under their rule—if we can take such a word to formalize their influence—some of the best twentieth-century poets received their rightful reputations.

The opinions and methods of these senior poets and critics were in time adopted by the majority of their successors among the scholars and teacher-critics of following generations; through the universities and journals they have made their ideas felt in literature as well as in literary studies. Therefore it is no shock to hear in later years stirrings of rejection and discontent on the one hand and outright explosions of rebellion on the other. "The restrictions of a benevolent tyranny" is what Donald Hall, in the introduction to his anthology *Contemporary American Poetry* (1962), has called the result of this rule. He continues: "For thirty years an orthodoxy ruled American poetry. It derived from the authority of T. S. Eliot and the new critics; it exerted itself through the literary quarterlies and the universities. It asked for a poetry of symmetry, intellect, irony, and wit." So, oddly enough, the poet whose radical vision gave birth to a highly experimental poem such as *The Waste Land* was used later by his interpreters as the authority to endorse those exercises in wit and the employment of myth—which all too soon turned drearily academic—as the stuff of which great poetry is made.

But this critical rulership, as Hall assuredly knows, always *seems* much more powerful than it really is, mainly because it holds positions in journals or institutions of learning. Though they may be compelled to labor in obscurity and neglect, writers will settle on independent courses in spite of critical dogmas and the fact that some of their fellows obey them. Surely one of the salutary features of American poetry is its tremendous diversity and the refusal by all good poets to bow to any rules but those they have freely chosen for themselves. Indeed, the Beatniks and the Hip poets have shown us that there is a side of the American literary imagination that wishes to escape rule, form, and reason altogether; that, at its limit, grows impatient with language and the very processes required of it. Given this diversity and the bewildering multiplicity of poets in this country—some in isolation, some in underground poetic movements or groups, some writing or publishing year by year in the "respectable" journals without forfeiting their aesthetic self-reliance—it is hard to believe that more than a surface layer of academicism has hardened over poetry in the past thirty years. Criticism is another subject—one in which we have no interest here.

The poets studied in this book all began to write during that span of thirty years cited by Hall; and I have put the word "contemporary" in my title rather than "modern" to separate them from the pioneer modernists of Eliot's generation and the slightly later poets of the 1920s. These "contemporary" poets arrived either in the wake of the modernist revolution (Eberhart, Kunitz, Roethke) or a good ten years or more after its finish. They have not enjoyed a mood of collective inspiration but, without the benefit of any shared aesthetic aim or revolutionary artistic goal, have had to cultivate voices on their own, making them distinctive by selecting for themselves models and guides both from earlier literature and from the pioneer modernists preceding them. Yet the difficulties of being a beginner in this period have involved more than the problems of writing good poems.

So attentive were the critics to the poetic upheavals of the modernists that they seldom heard these newer writers. In a very perceptive and moving tribute to the late Theodore Roethke, published in the *New York Review of Books*, Stanley Kunitz outlines the predicament of the contemporary poet in the aftermath of the modernist revolution:

> Immediately after Eliot and Pound and Hart Crane and Stevens and William Carlos Williams, to mention only a handful, it was difficult to be taken seriously as a new American poet; for the title to "the new poetry" was in the possession of a dynasty of extraordinary gifts and powers, not the least of which was its capacity for literary survival. When Roethke was a schoolboy in Michigan in the twenties, these poets had already "arrived." Today, in the general view, they are still the rebels and inventors beyond whom even a college course in contemporary literature scarcely dares to venture.

In spite of the disadvantageous places some excellent poets have been compelled to occupy and the unwarranted neglect experienced by too many of them, they were freed from the chores of literary revolt to devote themselves wholeheartedly to the creation of poems. And from contemporary poets young and old we have had, and are still having, a steady flow of the finest work, even though critical and public acclaim for the most part lags.

The studies in these next chapters, arranged in chronological order by the poets' birth dates, try to supply a partial corrective to the situation Stanley Kunitz describes by introducing the reader to a few of the accomplished and representative poets of the designated three decades. Thus the book begins with a trio of veteran figures—Eberhart, Kunitz, and Roethke—all of whom were hard at work in the early 1930s, though they gained public acknowledgment of their poetic success only in the late 1950s. Shapiro, Lowell, and Wilbur, younger men, came to be known more quickly in the years after the war. Brother Antoninus had to wait for the San Francisco Renascence (as it was sometimes called) to come into the general view. Elizabeth Bishop and Isabella Gardner have yet to be given the wider applause they deserve. Finally, Denise Levertov, James Wright, and Anne Sexton represent current tendencies in American poetry which foreshadow, I believe, important future developments; they are, moreover, very accomplished writers.

I

Richard Eberhart

What D. H. Lawrence wrote to his friend Catherine Carswell early in 1916 about the rudimentary qualities necessary to poetry in the modern world might easily have served as a prophetic description of the working rules behind the poetic practice of Richard Eberhart, whose first book appeared in England the year of Lawrence's death. Lawrence says in his letter, "The essence of poetry with us in this age of stark and unlovely actualities is a stark directness, without a shadow of a lie, or a shadow of deflection anywhere. Everything can go, but this stark, bare rocky directness, this alone makes poetry today." In keeping with the spirit of this dictum Eberhart is concerned throughout his poetry with revealing an experience as if it were happening at that very moment and had to be set down in all its directness, unadorned complexity, and innate lyricism—or be lost. The reader is seldom allowed to believe that any poem by Eberhart is the result of passion reconsidered or emotion recollected in tranquillity; only in his later work do we find any evidence of such calm. Though a poem may ostensibly treat an experience of the past, the tense of the verb means little or nothing; it is a grudging concession to practicality, for the experience, related with the breathless fury of an immediate sensation, occurs in a timeless *now*—an imaginative moment and space untouched by external measurements—and has an urgency that abolishes our temporal distinctions.

This characteristic, so fundamental to Eberhart's writing, can be seen in his widely anthologized poem "The Groundhog," which gives the impression of a suspended present, though there are time lapses and shifts, and though everything has already happened:

> In June, amid the golden fields,
> I saw a groundhog lying dead.
> Dead lay he; my senses shook,
> And mind outshot our naked frailty.
> There lowly in the vigorous summer
> His form began its senseless change,
> And made my senses waver dim
> Seeing nature ferocious in him.
> Inspecting close his maggots' might
> And seething cauldron of his being,
> Half with loathing, half with a strange love,
> I poked him with an angry stick.
> The fever arose, became a flame
> And Vigour circumscribed the skies,
> Immense energy in the sun,
> And through my frame a sunless trembling.
> My stick had done nor good nor harm.
> Then I stood silent in the day
> Watching the object, as before;
> And kept my reverence for knowledge
> Trying for control, to be still,
> To quell the passion of the blood;
> Until I had bent down on my knees
> Praying for joy in the sight of decay.
> And so I left; and I returned

In autumn strict of eye, to see
The sap gone out of the groundhog,
But the bony sodden hulk remained.
But the year had lost its meaning,
And in intellectual chains
I lost both love and loathing,
Mured up in the wall of wisdom.
Another summer took the fields again
Massive and burning, full of life,
But when I chanced upon the spot
There was only a little hair left,
And bones bleaching in the sunlight
Beautiful as architecture;
I watched them like a geometer,
And cut a walking stick from a birch.
It has been three years, now.
There is no sign of the groundhog.
I stood there in the whirling summer,
My hand capped a withered heart,
And thought of China and of Greece,
Of Alexander in his tent;
Of Montaigne in his tower,
Of Saint Theresa in her wild lament.

The discovery, departures, and returns are all clearly
indicated by the poet; and yet we scarcely distinguish
between them because he never permits the overwhelming immediacy of the entire process of decomposition to
escape our attention. We jump from one phase of decay
to the next with hardly a pause; only near the end of the
poem are we brought up short with the recognition of
time's passage. And then it is just for an instant before
the poet utters his passionate outcry of mind and heart
engendered by this experience. Thus the breaks in the
time sequence and the fact that the whole series of events
belongs to the past are forgotten in the dramatic state-

ment of experience in the poem. The occurrences of an
Eberhart poem, however we locate them in our familiar
temporal scheme, exist always in their own present tense
too, the tense which is the poem's.

The rough and uneven character of Richard Eberhart's
writing over the past thirty-five years, which has been so
frequently remarked upon both by admirers and detrac-
tors, is the inevitable consequence of his approach to
poetry and is rooted in his romantic, inspirational notion
of the poetic act. Unlike Eliot, Pound, or even Dylan
Thomas, he is apparently not a writer for whom exhaustive revision has much importance. I do not mean, of
course, that he never alters a word or emends a line—
certainly he does; but Eberhart's poems show little evidence of extensive revision. He preserves in books only
some of the poems published in journals and magazines.
In a way, though probably not consciously, he is hostile
to the idea of pure art, to the institution of literature.
With Walt Whitman, William Carlos Williams, James
Agee, Henry Miller, William Faulkner, and other American writers, he shares a distrust of writing that refuses
to submit itself to near-domination by the experience it
renders. For Whitman and Williams poetic form is
elicited from, rather than imposed upon, reality. Faulkner's novels, though elaborate in construction, are composed as though the simultaneous flow of thoughts and
events would engulf author and characters alike. Henry
Miller can retreat no further from his autobiography,
from the pressure of his life, than an occasional fantasy;
and Agee, in the prefatory comments to *Let Us Now
Praise Famous Men*, specifically disavows the artistic
purpose. The reality of experience matters most for these
writers: how to close the distance between book and occurrence.

The beginning of Eberhart's "Notes on Poetry," in
John Ciardi's *Mid-Century American Poets*, offers a
glimpse of his understanding of the poet's mental opera-

tions; these are largely determined, or so it seems, by forces and accidents outside his control:

> A poet does what he can do. Poetry is dynamic, Protean. In the rigors of composition it seems to me that the poet's mind is a filament informed with the irrational vitality of energy as it was discovered in our time in quantum mechanics. The quanta may shoot off any way. (You breathe in maybe God.)

These ideas hardly fit in with the theory of composition endorsed by the literary establishment of our day. Yet Eberhart is assuredly not so irrational in his writing as we might think from the above passage, and there are plenty of poems to prove it. However, I can imagine someone being stodgy and foolish enough to point to Eberhart's inspirational and vitalistic aesthetic, and then to his worst poetic failures, and expect you to see how—obviously—the one bred the other. But Eberhart's successes are dependent upon the same poetics. His art is always and everywhere idiosyncratic, and that accounts in part for its strength. At his peak he acquires an intensity of focus on his material that is matched by only a few of his contemporaries, such as Stanley Kunitz, Robert Lowell, and Theodore Roethke.

This poet turns a naked gaze on his experience and writes unreservedly from such perception. The surrender of himself to a luminous instant of vision and the momentous effort to seize it in words imbue Eberhart's poetry with its amazing power. Commitment, he so often tells us, should be to the truth, but we cannot from our limited and relative positions know truth fully. Therefore the poet must commit himself totally to "vision felt as absolute when experienced." The visionary perceptions that come to Eberhart may be prompted by something seen or undergone in the routine of daily living that suddenly discloses an inner or hidden meaning. In "New Hampshire, February," the poet discovers two wasps

wedged into a crevice of his house and nearly dead with
the cold. He removes them and places them in a pan,
then tries to revive them:

> Like God touching his finger to Adam
> I felt, and thought of Michaelangelo,
> For whenever I breathed on them,
> The slightest breath,
> They leaped, and preened as if to go.
>
> My breath controlled them always quite.
> More sensitive than electric sparks
> They came into life
> Or they withdrew to ice,
> While I watched, suspending remarks.
>
> Then one in a blind career got out,
> And fell to the kitchen floor. I
> Crushed him with my cold ski boot,
> By accident. The other
> Had not the wit to try or die.
>
> And so the other is still my pet.
> The moral of this is plain.
> But I will shirk it.
> You will not like it. And
> God does not live to explain.

Against this kind of despairing parable of existence,
which often forms in his mind out of reflection on the
seeming irrationality of happenings in the world, Eberhart sets other poems arising from meditation on abstract, religious, or ethical themes. In spite of the angry
skepticism with which the poem above closes, its moral
questioning is clear, substantial, and human; and in many
other poems answers are indirectly furnished to these
queries. The responses frequently border on religious
vision, partake of it, or further probe spiritual torment.

"Reality! Reality! What Is It?" makes a good example. As the poem begins, the poet confesses his denials of Christ and states his own position as that of a man who always "considered the first truth tragedy." This opening announcement is deftly altered from stanza to stanza as the poem proceeds, and the finish reaches an unexpected pitch of religious emotion:

> O Christ of Easter, impossible Man, Lord, and
>   God
> I, cold geographer, map Your clear estate
> As one sentient, yet a prisoner, clashing Thy
> Cymbal in the gliding sound of my dying.
>
> Christ of Christ, what are you, beast or God,
> Must I deny that sweat upon that cross?
> Must I affirm whatever is not what I am,
> Christ, Christ! reality! reality! what is it?

The contradictory nature of the attitudes taken in these two poems, the first from *Burr Oaks* (1947), the second from *Undercliff* (1953), should not baffle the reader, for the forcefulness of Eberhart's poetry depends upon his fidelity to the inwardness of his moods, inspirations, and perceptions; but he rejects the idea of systematizing them, lest their essential truth be warped or lost. His practice may seem less inconsistent after we have read more than a few of his poems and have begun to notice a recurrence of interests: the attempt to achieve moments of vision; the balancing against one another of intellect and emotion; the constant questioning of death; the probing of the limits of reality.

In the course of his career Eberhart's poetry and his conception of it have not changed radically but have simply been tempered and modified. The concluding poem ("The Incomparable Light") of his collected edition still admits a fundamental tentativeness and a reluctance to name definitely the covert sources of poetic vision:

Elusive element, final mystery,
The light beyond compare has been my visitant,
Some sort of angel sometimes at my shoulder,
A beckoning guide, elusive nevertheless . . .

We think at once here of Rilke and his personally devised
angelology, but how different is Eberhart's evasive statement—withdrawn as it is made—from the bold and em-
phatic presence of angels in the German poet's *Duino
Elegies*. All the same, Eberhart now tends more and
more consistently to place the origin of his perceptions
in a realm beyond mere physical appearance, a realm that
is spiritual if not as yet plainly mapped. In the verse play
Devils and Angels, included in Eberhart's *Collected
Verse Plays* (1962), a character closely resembling the
poet is visited by an angel and hears of the influence of
such a realm upon the lesser human one. The angel says,

I come to bring you harmony and serenity,
To remind you of a height beyond your condition,
I have come like a blinding of the insight,
Those times you have had in the night without
     words,
Or in the day beyond care; those inner reaches
Of your spirit, when you dreamed beyond death;
Those hours of meditation on a mountain,
Those endless moments of perception in daydream;
Those apparently unreal and disjointed times
When you felt the world as an immaculate
     radiance
In the hand of God; in those incredible intuitions
I was always there, beneficent and without harm
     to you.

However, his genuine visionary propensities never divorce
Eberhart from an abiding attachment to the human estate, though his poems lean now in one of these directions, now in the other, and sometimes combine them.

The earliest of Eberhart's works, A *Bravery of Earth* (1930), is a book-length autobiographical narrative poem from which the author has wisely preserved only a few lovely lyrical passages like the beautiful "This fevers me, this sun on green." The poem, though personal, attempts to surpass any restrictions of privacy and seeks the general theme of youth and an awakening to the world, to love and sensual pleasure, which is followed by a fall from this ecstatic innocence into the disillusionment caused by the knowledge of death. The last, and best, section of the poem recounts the young poet's travels as a steamer hand to China. Here Eberhart conveys his narrative with objectivity and purpose, although the previous parts are often swamped by undisciplined language and confused emotions. Even in a work of this length Eberhart sustains a frenzied note, and the poem rushes from beginning to end at breakneck pace. It is, at best, an immature poem, but it reveals immediately the poet's fascination with the dualities of experience: his desire to embrace equally the perpetual conflicts of reason with feeling, skepticism with belief, spirit with matter.

His audacious handling of language is, from the start, also characteristic, though he shows much greater inventiveness and dexterity in his second book, *Reading the Spirit*. Edwin Muir once suggested that Eberhart wrote as if he had encountered words for the first time. Nothing could be more correct. He approaches language with naiveté and freshness; in his frequent disregard for common linguistic usage he employs words as things, hurling them at the reader's senses and consciousness in an ordered bombardment that forces new meanings from apparently intractable material, or that bursts with sudden, unearthly light. Of course the same spontaneous usage causes the faults, the errors in taste which flaw too many poems that might, with some care, have been saved. This notion of composition demands of the poet that he catch an experience in words as it comes to him, not afterwards by reconstruction. Whatever the poem is, it is an attempted seizure of that experience, not an effort to duplicate it from memory. Eberhart resembles D. H. Lawrence in this poetic intention—though I am pointing to a similarity of inspiration rather than an influence—for Lawrence's interest was in snatching the fleeting moment from oblivion in its natural state. But Eberhart's poems read differently from Lawrence's, and in his finest early pieces the sense of the words constituting the experience creates startling results; sometimes, as in "When Golden Flies Upon My Carcass Come," we are reminded of the witty and paradoxical manner of Donne or Marvell:

> When golden flies upon my carcass come,
> Those pretty monsters, shining globules
> Like tautened oily suns, and congregate
> Fixing their several gems upon one core
> That shines a blossom then of burning gold,
> 'Tis as the sun's burning glass and diadem
> They work, at the first chance of rotten flesh,
> And, senseless little messengers of time,
> Some beauty keep even at the guts of things,
> Which is a fox caught, and I watch the flies.

Eberhart's language and syntax are the most obviously striking properties of his verse; and this is as it should be, for they reflect more than anything else his conception of poetry and also embody his individual vision of reality.

In autobiographical poems such as A *Bravery of Earth*, later short poems like "Orchard" and "The Soul Longs to Return Whence It Came," as well as in the play *The Visionary Farms* and the brief sketch of his life written for Stanley Kunitz' *Twentieth Century Authors*, Eberhart notes particular events that undoubtedly had a direct bearing on his view of experience and on various aspects of his poetic temperament. Born into a family of means in Minnesota, Eberhart appears to have faced a period during his youth when tragedy struck wholesale at his family. His mother died of cancer, and his father, a stalwart and reliable man, suffered grave business reversals. The poet has often returned to the subject of his mother's illness, her constancy in the grip of mortal disease, and his ensuing grief, which was an introduction to the world of adult life. "Orchard," which takes this illness as its subject, begins with a family auto ride to visit a grove of fruit trees at dusk. The air is permeated with fear and horror—of the known for the parents, of the unknown for the children—whose causes are only gradually extended to us:

> Lovely were the fruit trees in the evening.
> We sat in the automobile all five of us,
> Full of the silence of deep grieving,
> For tragedy stalked among the fruit trees.
>
> Strongest was the father, of solid years,
> Who set his jaw against the coming winter,
> Pure, hard, strong, and infinitely gentle
> For the worst that evil brings can only kill us.
>
> Most glorious was the mother, beautiful
> Who in the middle course of life was stalked
> By the stark shape of malignant disease,
> And her face was holy white like all desire.
>
> And we three, in our benumbing youngness,
> Half afraid to guess at the danger there,
> Looked in stillness at the growing fruit trees,
> While tumultuous passions raged in the air.

Eberhart achieves here a curious ambivalence in his attitude, for the occasion is witnessed half with the innocent eye of a child, half with the wisdom acquired from living—the sort of combination we might associate with Blake's earlier poems. The second part of the poem focuses on the strength of the father, the mother's capac-

ity for love, and "the first light/Of brutal recognition"
the three children receive. At the conclusion the entire
orchard has been transformed into a scene of turbulent
and conflicting passions. The people themselves are
nearly obscured, as ships and men are in a Turner painting of a storm at sea; forces are unleashed in what has
now almost become an abstract realm of spirit:

> And in the evening, among the warm fruit trees
> All of life and all of death were there,
> Of pain unto death, of struggle to endure,
> And the strong right of human love was there.

One could criticize these lines for loosening their hold
on tangible actuality, yet the passage makes clear Eberhart's moral impulse and his desire to connect the tragic
situation of the family with universal conditions of suffering and of virtue. The somewhat abstract dimension
presents it as a manifestation of a much larger struggle.

A sensitivity to death, to its eruption in the midst of
a full existence, haunts Eberhart's poetry and stems, at
least partially, from this bitter childhood circumstance.
Yet we never find in the poems a fear of death as such.
Sometimes death exerts a spell over the poet's imagination; at other times it seems merely an unwelcome intrusion on life or a means of humiliating man. In visionary
poems such as "A Meditation" and "Imagining How It
Would Be To Be Dead" Eberhart even tries to project
himself—with differing effects—beyond the boundaries
of life. He has adjusted to the idea of death without
succumbing to the sort of obsession with it that fills the
atmosphere of, say, Dylan Thomas' work.

Along with the realization of suffering and death—and
the quiet heroism with which they may be met—Eberhart discovered the facts of time, change, and determinacy. The contrary attitudes so noticeable from poem to
poem, especially in his earlier writings, illustrate his basic
contention that our experience of reality is an experience

of opposites, and that of them is life composed. Eberhart sees his artistic task as one of exploring, through seizures of intuition, his own nature and that of the world together. Thus in what amounts to a search for the truth of all existence—a truth he is wise enough to know he cannot hope to grasp—the poet must not be, he argues, "a dogmatist"; he needs rather to be "a relativist." (*Twentieth Century Authors, First Supplement,* p. 298.) Knowledge and experience are fragmentary; we have not "perfect understanding" of our condition. Poetry—particularly, one gathers, if it comes from a stroke of spiritual insight—is a gesture toward understanding, an advance toward the unity and perfection we believe is ours by some right but which we still do not know. Eberhart writes in his "Notes on Poetry":

> The motive for writing is to make up for some sense of lack in oneself, an obscure and earthly realization that must be old as man. This includes, of course, the excess of energy common to the artist, his direct and violent perception. Divisive man can know unity only at death (or so he can speculate), and he cannot know what kind of unity that is. He lives in continuous struggle with his imperfection and the imperfection of life. If one were only conscious of harmony, there would be no need to write.

Whatever indecisiveness remains in Eberhart's mind, his thinking and writing, as Michael Roberts says in the preface to *Reading the Spirit* (1936), have their foundation in the main ideas of the Christian tradition. Another excerpt from "Notes on Poetry" points up the author's sense of original sin—or its results—the broken experience of life which poetry tries to reassemble. "Christ is the poem absolute," he writes, and is thus "impossible to overhaul," because He incarnates a beauty, harmony, and ordered love beyond man's ordinary capacities. Poems will at least open such possibilities of love and order to contemplation, though as poems they cannot in themselves provide those qualities lacking in our lives.

Some critics have spoken of a resemblance to Wallace Stevens in some of Eberhart's more recent poems. A superficial resemblance is visible at times, but nothing more than that. Eberhart never shows any inclination to subscribe to Stevens' theory of the imagination, nor does he share Stevens' tendency to deify this human faculty. Many of his poems register the mind's lyrical impulse raised to feverish heights by the imperfection of things, by the destructive element at work in the reality we inhabit, or by visions of the transcendent and ideal. Stevens' poetry elaborates an aesthetic system with which to view the world; Eberhart accepts reality as he finds it, or as it is given to him, with all its contradictions (this does not preclude his moral judgment, which will be discussed presently):

> It is a terrible thrall to be alone,
> With all joy there, and destroying fate
> Slicing the flesh, hot fangs on the bone;
> The intense quality of desire
> Blasphemes, and is at fault to the core.
> Silence in bitterness is the hardest thing;
> But nobler to ask the fire to burn more,
> If the mind can endure, and can sing.
> Even beyond joy and despair are spun
> Unutterable remoteness in the air,
> Intolerable nearness in the sun,
> And the separateness of each man in his lair.
>   ("Necessity")

These lines, and many others in Eberhart's poetry, describe, among a variety of things, a release from the confinements of ordinary perception made available to the poet by intuition or inspiration. The final worth of these luminous moments—"seer-states," Eberhart calls them—consists in the light they shower on the extremities of human life, because they allow the one who is visited by them to transcend the enervating conflicts and paradoxes of his normal situation as a man and to touch a spiritual region of freedom and unity. Even though the attitudes held in different poems may clash, each is true to the insight that made it possible. The poet cannot, of course, remain on this exalted plane, since he has not the human capacity to withstand its pressures. T. S. Eliot gives us in "Burnt Norton" one of the best reminders that timeless experience must be followed by a return to the temporal:

> Yet the enchainment of past and future
> Woven in the weakness of the changing body,
> Protects mankind from heaven and damnation
> Which flesh cannot endure.

Eberhart is less orthodox in his view than Eliot, though the idea here applies to both poets. The late Joseph Warren Beach said of Eberhart that he was "mystic" but never strict in any doctrinal adherence, and this summary remark is accurate. So we find Eberhart writing in *Twentieth Century Authors*, "A poet has to be two persons, at least two. He has to have superior energies, enough for the world as it is, in which he does not believe, and an abundance for the world of becoming, which he makes real."

Poetry, then, is frequently for Eberhart an overthrowing of things as they are in order to get to things as they *really* are—that is, beyond illusion or mere appearance. However, it would be a misinterpretation of his work to think of it as the result of a close apprehension of the Divine, and the poet makes no such pretense. Poems often grow out of vision and lightning flashes of profound spiritual intuition, yet these do not resolve Eberhart's uncertainties, which are as central to his inner life as they are to his art.

While he is a visionary poet, Eberhart never denies the substantial weight of the world, of its actual presence, though his comments are sometimes in conflict with his poems. Thus if he is a visionary, he is almost always a strong moralist as well. He continues to insist upon human finitude, fallibility, and blindness as limitations of existence. As a religious or visionary poet he attacks the bounds of knowledge, not in the hope of soaring completely free of the world but to report to men his discoveries. With his French contemporary, René Char, he views the poet as "the source of a being that projects and preserves." His poem " 'The Goal of Intellectual Man' " clarifies the larger purposes of Eberhart's visionary poetry forcefully and compassionately:

> The goal of intellectual man
> Striving to do what he can
> To bring down out of uncreated light
> Illumination to our night
>
> Is not possession of the fire
> Annihilation of his own desire
> To the source a secret soaring
> And all his self outpouring
>
> Nor is it an imageless place
> Wherein there is no human face
> Nor laws, nor hierarchies, nor dooms
> And only the cold weight of the tomb
>
> But it is human love, love
> Concrete, specific, in a natural move
> Gathering goodness, it is free
> In the blood as in the mind's harmony,
>
> It is love discoverable here
> Difficult, dangerous, pure, clear,

The truth of the positive hour
Composing all of human power.

This love becomes a motive strength informing most of Eberhart's poetry; and poetry in its turn, which is "not less than an attempt to move the world, to order the chaos of man," has definite ends to achieve by its transforming powers: "love, harmony, order; poise, precision, new worlds." (*Twentieth Century Authors, First Supplement*, p. 298.) The aesthetic experience does not exist apart from the impurities of life, for love, if it is honest and deep, creates distinctions and judgments, and rises into anger at the sight of man's failure to be what he can or what he pretends to be. At this point Eberhart's personal lyricism blends with his public view: the visionary intention and the moral come together.

Among the best commentators on Eberhart, James Hall and Selden Rodman have noted the poet's moral, even didactic, stance in numerous poems. Such a stance is occasionally quite effective, though it can also be strained, flat, or awkward. (See, for example, "Letter I" or "Fragment of New York, 1929," from *Undercliff: Poems 1946-1953*.) In any event, moral judgment springs naturally from the urgency with which Eberhart writes, an urgency not so common in contemporary poetry. Outrage and protest at human conduct, its folly and brutality, generate "World War," "At the End of War," "Fragment of New York, 1929," "Aesthetics after War," and other poems in which the author's control over his material is constantly threatened by his emotions driving forward into speech:

What has aesthetics to do with society?
Was the Italian airman crazy
When he saw aesthetic purity
In bombs flowering like roses a mile below?
He could not see nor feel the pain of man.

Our own men testify to awe,
If not to aesthetic charm,
On seeing man's total malice over Hiroshima,
That gigantic, surrealistic, picture mushroom
And objectification of megalomania.
A world of men who butcher men
In the arsenical best interests of several states,
The modern warring maniacal man,
Is this world of men inimical
To the postulates of the study aesthetics?

("Aesthetics after War")

Our answer to Eberhart's question must be a qualified
assent. And with that question the poet seems also to be
asking and replying to its corollary: is poetry possible in
our present state of affairs? The lack of stylistic concern
and the anger with which the passage is written lead us
to think the response would be negative. But again it
needs qualification, for Eberhart has given a lifetime to
the practice of poetry; and yet we feel quite rightly, along
with him, that the thought of art or craft collapses before the horror and bestiality of much of our contemporary experience. Impatience with the rigors of craft is ex-
cusable enough under these circumstances, and other
poets such as Rexroth, Ciardi, and Rukeyser have surely
felt it too. In Eberhart's case we know also that the
rendering of immediate emotion is consistent with his
poetics.

Writing in the present age wants frequently to be
more than writing, if I may put it that way—a weapon
of disgust, dismay, indignation, love, and justice. These
demands do not appear completely unwarranted when
literature is severed from most institutional and communal support, from a shared philosophical or theological background, with the exception of what it provides
for itself. At the extreme limits of this situation, and in
the midst of conflict and death, literary values may be

held only by sheer chance so far as the writer is concerned; he will not necessarily seek them out. Yet the fact remains that Eberhart, like most other poets, wins his truly compelling effects when his feelings are constrained by an order of language, by obvious care, and then are permitted to expand their meanings within the reader's consciousness. We prize that quality in Robert Lowell's and Stanley Kunitz' verse, and in some of the fiercest poems of Randall Jarrell, Theodore Roethke, and James Wright; and it is Eberhart's quality in his very best work—such a poem as "The Fury of Aerial Bombardment," for one:

> You would think the fury of aerial bombard-
> ment
> Would rouse God to relent; the infinite spaces
> Are still silent. He looks on shock-pried faces.
> History, even, does not know what is meant.
>
> You would feel that after so many centuries
> God would give man to repent; yet he can kill
> As Cain could, but with multitudinous will,
> No farther advanced than in his ancient furies.
>
> Was man made stupid to see his own stupidity?
> Is God by definition indifferent, beyond us all?
> Is the eternal truth man's fighting soul
> Wherein the beast ravens in its own avidity?
>
> Of Van Wettering I speak, and Averill,
> Names on a list, whose faces I do not recall
> But they are gone to early death, who late in
> school
> Distinguished the belt feed lever from the belt
> holding pawl.

The inhumanity of war occupies Eberhart in a number of poems from *Burr Oaks*, and his *Selected Poems* (1951) includes the narrative poem "The Brotherhood of Men," one of his most successful longer pieces. The speaker, an American soldier, is captured by the Japanese at Corregidor and made to participate in the "death march" which ends with his shipment to Japan as a prisoner. Shipwrecked but recaptured, he finally reaches his destination, where he is imprisoned until the close of the war. Details are graphic and describe with awesome and fearful suggestion the reduction of life to barely human rudiments—and even these daily dwindle away. The survivor acquires, of necessity, the self-protective device of a certain hardness of mind, a psychology of perseverance. But Eberhart finds more in the telling of this story than the brutal enumeration of facts; the experience, almost exceeding our capacity for belief were we not so familiar with its many counterparts in the history of the last decades, serves as a lesson to those who do survive and can reflect upon it. The narrator is capable of drawing from the human evil and waste, the intolerable suffering, a value, now ground into the prisoners' very flesh and bones, inscribed upon their hearts:

> And yet I know (a knowledge unspeakable)
> That we were at our peak when in the depths,
> Lived close to life when cuffed by death,
> Had visions of brotherhood when we were broken,
> Learned compassion beyond the curse of passion,
> And never in after years those left to live
> Would treat with truth as in those savage times,
> And sometimes wished that they had died
> As did those many crying in their arms.

A sense of humanity fills Eberhart's poems, even when most abstract and speculative; for this reason more than any other he requires a moral answer to his questioning of our condition, however unsatisfactory or inadequate that answer might, at times, be. The lines above have their analogues everywhere in the events of this era. In addressing himself to such matters Eberhart parallels with his narrative poem the aims of Camus in *The Plague* or Faulkner in *A Fable*. The ordeal of suffering burns and tortures but purifies the vision, lifts the ideal into sight. "Art," Eberhart writes in his "Notes on Poetry," "is essentially social."

Poetry as knowledge, poetry as power—between these two tendencies Eberhart has divided his art. The poems that capture in all their suddenness and gratuitousness moments of illumination do not in any way contradict those moral essays that call to account human motives and actions. Each aspect of his verse complements and enriches the other. What counts in both is the instantaneous, sharp, and piercing vision, and its expression: the words which create an experience because they are of its essence and are not an afterthought.

An association with the earth and a persistent affection for the forms and details of nature give many of Eberhart's poems a point of departure and return. From the early *A Bravery of Earth* and "Four Lakes' Days" to some of his newest poems in *The Quarry* (1964) that association never weakens. On numerous occasions it is a cause for joy and exaltation—not unlike the feelings of Wordsworth and Coleridge—an awareness of human ties with creation or simply a recognition of freedom. His eye for nature's particulars does not depend on an interest in appearances alone so much as it does on a wish to read in them something more than just tree or bush or stream. Nature can open to the poet a hidden reserve of spiritual energies:

> Go to the shine that's on a tree
> When dawn has laved with liquid light
> With luminous light the nighted tree
> And take that glory without fright.

Go to the song that's in a bird
When he has seen the glistening tree,
That glorious tree the bird has heard
Give praise for its felicity.

Then go to the earth and touch it keen,
Be tree and bird, be wide aware
Be wild aware of light unseen,
And unheard song along the air.
("Go to the Shine That's on a Tree")

This kind of experience also belongs to the measure
and intensity of visionary perception as Eberhart understands it. But if his imagination is touched by the invisible, the single means by which it may be conveyed is
the visible. The poet's researches of the spirit are thus
held in check by physical reality and by the sensual qualities of words. Looking at Eberhart's poetry altogether,
one thinks of a long succession of personal meditations
beginning in specific instances: the thought of death; the
public actualities of our time; the meanings latent in a
place, an object, a memory. Any one of these could
provoke thought and revelation; yet wherever his fertile
imagination, as a result, might lead him, he stays partially anchored to the concrete source from which he began. So he writes at the conclusion of "Autumnal," one
of his later poems:

What is going on beyond
I have not found, am bound
To the love of the unfound
Beyond, but here.

Eberhart's enduring conviction of the human and
moral purpose in his poetry confers a distinctive unity
upon it. His belief enables him to hold in a single vision
of life the disparities of experience: the feelings of ela-
tion along with those of pessimism; the knowledge of

God with the fear of a final emptiness; the revulsion at evil with the pleasure in goodness and beauty. These antithetical attitudes are the inheritance of all men, not merely of the poet. In whatever way Eberhart's writings are examined, his aesthetics demands first a meaning for man—a challenge to his situation in the world; a truth extracted from the disorder of things. If the answers and lessons the poet supplies sometimes oppose one another, they still maintain a veracity to the predicaments from which they were born. Eberhart never flinches at what he sees; in "The Passage," from the *Collected Poems*, he correctly calls his poetic insight "a gift of the true."

II

Stanley Kunitz

Literary reputations are curious and unsettling phantoms; they come and go like restless spirits, blown by dark winds of chance and influence. Quiet attention to craft, long and careful research into experience and the methods of expressing it, devotion to craft before fame —these are indeed rare virtues at any time and frequently they receive small reward. Such distinguishing marks have been evident for more than three decades in the poetry of Stanley Kunitz, and it is one of the disturbing facts of our contemporary literary life that this poet only recently began to gain the reception and the following he had so long deserved. Robert Lowell could say very truthfully that the appearance of Kunitz' *Selected Poems* in 1958 made him "the poet of the hour," for it brought belated recognition to one of the strongest and most energetic talents in American poetry.

Kunitz' output has not been large; the selected volume, which covers thirty years, numbers only 116 pages. Before this book he had published just two other collections of verse: *Intellectual Things* (1931) and *Passport to the War* (1944). The table of contents of *Selected Poems* shows the scrupulous process of screening to which the author has characteristically submitted his work. An ample portion of the first book has been discarded—was, in fact, discarded in the second half of *Passport to the War*, where he included the earlier poems he apparently wished to preserve. One may readily lament this perhaps unduly harsh self-criticism, but it is the poet's right and is fully in keeping with the demands of perfection Kunitz so obviously makes upon himself. Again, in *Selected Poems* Kunitz has shuffled poems around and has grouped them under thematic headings. However, his themes have changed with time and his later manner has relaxed a little, so our approach to him in the following pages will occasionally justify chronological comments.

A reading of only a few scattered poems might lead one to believe that Kunitz is a writer of complicated occasional verse, a poetry dictated by outside occurrences, given over to capturing the isolated and particular moods or responses they evoke, and bound together by a uniform complexity of language. But this sort of reading would miss the forceful impression of a singular artistic mind on the raw material of these poems and the consequent realization that their main theme is the struggle of that very mind with the experience it comes up against. Having read the bulk of Kunitz' work, we recognize that his poetic intelligence and imaginative strength are not subservient to external occasions, but that, on the contrary, the poem is itself an occasion resulting from the tremendous pressures of the writer's psyche and his passionate feelings in contact with the processes of life. Although his later poetry more often takes in the public world of our time, it too is cast in the mirror-images of an interior state.

In "The Science of the Night," Kunitz begins with a conventional domestic or amatory circumstance, and with the diction and tone appropriate to gentle affections; but this intimacy merely spurs him to depart into more dar-

ing speculation. The poet, awake in the middle of the
night, muses on the comfort of the woman beside him,
until the adjectives of the poem's third line break off
the emotion in a sudden reversal of intention which carries everything in another direction:

> I touch you in the night, whose gift was you,
> My careless sprawler,
> And I touch you cold, unstirring, star-bemused,
> That are become the land of your self-strangeness.

The lines that follow view sleep as an escape from the
reality of self and personality in one closely known. The
dreaming beloved turns into an explorer of vast and distant spaces; and the poet has forced upon him an understanding of the irrational, fleeting character of the individual, who slips uncontrollably away to hidden places,
there to partake of other lives, to inhabit other worlds:

> And even should I track you to your birth
> Through all the cities of your mortal trial,
> As in my jealous thought I try to do,
> You would escape me—from the brink of earth
> Take off to where the lawless auroras run,
> You with your wild and metaphysic heart.
> My touch is on you, who are light years gone.
> We are not souls but systems, and we move
> In clouds of our unknowing
>
> > like great nebulae.

Science and psychology, both prominent and influential in Kunitz' writing, replace the outward considerations of conjugal love. Next, the poet proceeds to examine a mythical analogy. Like Adam, from whose rib God
formed Eve, he feels a profound connection with the
woman who lies by him (the physical juxtaposition of
their bodies in the poem creates a metaphorical identification) but is nevertheless remote; and by virtue of this
bond he calls her back from sleep. Some lines near the

end request her awakening and gifts from her journeys. Then the poet discloses his position as the opposite of hers:

> My whirling hands stay at the noon,
> Each cell within my body holds a heart
> And all my hearts in unison strike twelve.

Noon and midnight, male and female, reason and unreason: these are the contrasting poles about which the poem takes shape. An extreme tension results from the simultaneous pull toward order and disorder, and is noticeable in the straining energy of the language, which tries to loosen itself from formal restrictions but is guided by the poet's steady purposiveness of thought. He seems more interested in where that thought will ultimately lead him than in the situation with which it all began. Since what he has written is not really a love poem so much as a meditation on the *unknowable* in even the closest relations, we are inclined to think of the domestic scene at the beginning as initiating a train of images and thoughts of which it is simply an appropriate vehicle. This does not mean that the poem lacks unity, but that its strength and aims are inward.

This poem, a rather recent one, indicates, as many earlier pieces do, the manner in which Kunitz very commonly utilizes an experience or event as the starting point for poetic reflection. His intelligence and imagination inform the material; diction, tone, and the movement of characteristic rhythms help to fashion Kunitz' own voice. We discover in his work a true poetic personality which, T. S. Eliot's distinction aside, both suffers and creates in the same act of composition. Kunitz is not committed to epistemological problems as Wallace Stevens was, and though there are sometimes faint traces of Yeats' influence in a turn of phrase or a rhythm here or there, he does not write under the protection of a mythological scheme as that great Irish poet did. Rather he reminds us of the secular Donne, occasionally of Marvell, and in certain ways of Baudelaire and Dylan Thomas. Jean Hagstrum in a fine essay on Kunitz in *Poets in Progress* has shown the consistent employment of anatomical imagery, of surgical and destructive metaphors. The human body is forever being dismembered, dissolved, or shrivelled up in Kunitz' poems, and he has himself remarked that "the hard and inescapable phenomenon to be faced is that we are living and dying at once" (*New World Writing*, 20). Here is a representative passage from "Postscript," an early poem. The poet, trying to flee the inexorable "progress" of things, is still caught on "time's acute/And bitter needle." The end is not an enviable one:

> Crueler than a spine
> It penetrates the body till it pricks
> The bubbling brain, exploding life's gray tumor
> Together with its iridescent world.

Kunitz exposes himself without benefit of philosophical theory, firm religious convictions, or any other strict system of absolute beliefs to the furious onslaught of experience, "a bewildering density," he calls it, "an overlay of episodes and images, both public and private," and to the awful loneliness and guilt that accompanies knowledge in the twentieth century. A poem for him appears to be an enforced reconciliation of his own basic emotions with his extremely sensitive perception of the realities he meets. He brings the strongest instruments at his disposal—reason and stoicism—to order these realities within himself. To the instruments named should be added love and its symbol, the poet's heart:

> O child,
> From my angry side
> Tumbles this agate heart,

> Your prize, veined with the root
> Of guilty life,
> From which flow love and art.
> (" 'What Have You Done?' ")

Knowledge and perception can defeat the natural attempts to view experience reasonably; and logic fails to withstand the passionate responses which well up in the poet. The tragic element in Kunitz' art often emerges from the collapse of reason before overwhelming odds. Such is the matter of another early poem, "Geometry of Moods," in which he traces the failure and destruction of a cosmological view, orderly and rational in its make-up through a fantastic pattern of imagery. The poem begins with a narrator who sees himself at the center of a number of universal spheres:

> Concentrical, the universe and I
> Rotated on God's crystal axletree,
>
> So perfectly adjusted in suspense
> I could not mark our split circumference,
>
> But sphere in sphere, devotion in devotion,
> Was a thing of folding air, a windy motion.

Purposely enough, it would seem, this cosmology of traditional origins grows more and more difficult to visualize; and we note that the tense in these lines is past: a *previous* state is being described. "Split circumference" likewise suggests the cracks and divisions in this whole to become evident later on. As the poem continues, the narrator outlines the essential features of man's spiritual anatomy which connect him—"My spinal pole, tipped with a globe of light"—with a world beyond the reaches of time—"Stretched long as time into the infinite." From his elevated position he looks back at earth, "love's in-

carnate form," which acts as a base and rest for the spirit
in its exercise of comprehending the universe. Earth appears finally to be a transparent circle with man at its
middle (this image is undoubtedly derived by Kunitz
from the Ptolemaic system), but such spareness and
purity of construction bring it dangerously close to the
great emptiness of space in which it floats:

> I core of the world, a bead in a ball of glass
> So pure that only nothing could be less.

In the last two stanzas the security of this universal
plan has very obviously become a thing of the past and
exists now only in memory, for the poem has shifted
abruptly into the present tense, dispersing the whole cosmic arrangement and leaving a lame, fragmentary residue
still in operation:

> Oh how the earth ensphered me, liberal and
>   warm,
> When the curve of heaven was her sleeping arm.
>
> Now cubical upon a fractured pole
> It creaks, scraping the circle of my soul.

What has actually happened to cause this failure we are
never told; but the change from faith in a universal system founded and supported by God, with man in its
highest place, to the experience of disbelief and of a disordered universe occurs in the transition from past to
present marked by the two stanzas above. Yet we must
not overlook the fact that in this representative poem of
Kunitz' something does survive the general ruin—"the
circle of my soul." And this soul may be said to harbor
those qualities we have already mentioned as this poet's
essential equipment, that is, his reason, conscience, heart,
individual integrity, and imagination. Together they raise
a constant bulwark of stoicism and affirm the notion of
a self that prevails even after the conflagration of experi-

ence; a self tormented by the desire to discover a truth
underlying the vicissitudes of life.

This self is the primary object of focus in the poems
of *Intellectual Things.* Armed with few presuppositions,
it is purged and toughened in the heated ovens of existence but never burned away. Its chief means of resist-
ance is the making of poems that aim to lend form and
significance to the arduousness of events, psychic or physical, by transforming them into words. In one way or another this process so intrigues Kunitz and is so much a
part of his mode of self-preservation that he treats it as
the subject or partial subject of some of his poems, for
example, " "What Have You Done?" " "Night Letter,"
and "Hermetic Poem." The last demonstrates the open
concern for his art that Kunitz has long shared with his
contemporaries:

> The secret my heart keeps
> Flows into cracked cups.
>
> No saucer can contain
> This overplus of mine:
>
> It glisters to the floor,
> Lashing like lizard fire
>
> And ramps upon the walls
> Crazy with ruby ills.
>
> Who enters by my door
> Is drowned, burned, stung, and starred.

The secret of the heart referred to consists primarily
of all the images and feelings stored up and mixed together in the poet as the result of his encounters with
the external world. Fermented by the imagination, these
are poured into the forms of art which do not entirely
subdue them, so that they leap forth to ravish the reader.

Kunitz' poem is a practical application of its thesis, and my account must therefore remain an oversimplification of the creative activity, though it does sketch, I believe, the poet's main idea. Poetic language under the conditions implied by this poem is stretched to the snapping point by the surge of emotions pressing against it. What Jean Hagstrum speaks of as Kunitz' "imagistic surrealism" accurately describes this phenomenon. Let us quote one more poem, "Open the Gates," with its more obvious nightmare effects, to exhibit the precision of Hagstrum's term in the "overplus" of feeling aroused by this short, bizarre narrative with its hauntingly suggestive words and images:

> Within the city of the burning cloud,
> Dragging my life behind me in a sack,
> Naked I prowl, scourged by the black
> Temptation of the blood grown proud.
>
> Here at the monumental door,
> Carved with the curious legend of my youth,
> I brandish the great bone of my death,
> Beat once therewith and beat no more.
>
> The hinges groan: a rush of forms
> Shivers my name, wrenched out of me.
> I stand on the terrible threshold, and I see
> The end and the beginning in each other's arms.

From his lonely kernel of *conscience* (to use the French word which means both "conscience" and "consciousness") Kunitz must try to develop a way of approaching life, a source of authority, for he has little else on which to rely. The figure of a woman in many poems helps to sustain him from without; and in "Father and Son" he searches through a dream landscape for his gentle but long dead father. But the end of his pursuit leaves him stunned with his terrifying independence:

At the water's edge, where the smothering ferns
    lifted
Their arms, "Father," I cried, "Return! You know
The way. I'll wipe the mudstains from your
    clothes;
No trace, I promise, will remain. Instruct
Your son, whirling between two wars,
In the Gemara of your gentleness,
For I would be a child to those who mourn
And brother to the foundlings of the field
And friend of innocence and all bright eyes.
O teach me how to work and keep me kind."

Among the turtles and the lilies he turned to me
The white ignorant hollow of his face.

Kunitz' skepticism and agnosticism are familiar attitudes
in modern writing; and he is not graced with the persistent heterodox mystical intuitions of Theodore Roethke
or Richard Eberhart. His vision at its deepest is generally
a revelation of death and apocalypse with neither explanation nor promise, though there are moments of rebirth
to a new plane of being within the self. But every venture
to the outer rim of human existence—see, for example,
"For the Word Is Flesh" and "Father and Son"—hurls
him back to the tumultuous core of that existence; there
he has to seek his answers. These are not the only limitations under which he works, for the self is incessantly
stricken by its own pangs of guilt, or what Kunitz metaphorically calls the "wound." Affliction of this kind may
be partially redeemed (it is, however, recurrent) through
continuous self-examination and the assertion of a few
fundamental beliefs: in the value of art and of human
relationships, in love and moral courage. Yet even these
are challenged in his brilliant and terrible poem "The
Surgeons," where Kunitz personifies in the figures of
operating surgeons the diabolical powers of the modern

world threatening human individuality and freedom.
Once again a poem assumes the aspect of a horrible but
inescapable dream, populated with men of "medicine"
who cut away the living substance of their patients:

> My surgeons are a savage band,
> Surely their patient is ill-fated.
> Their tricks are coarse: the small sweet hand
> I seized was wax, or amputated.
> With the humiliated swollen-footed
> And the lost persecuted their traps are baited.
>
> Deftly they opened the brain of a child,
> And it was full of flying dreams;
> Father was prowling in a field
> With speckled tongue and a collar of flame.
> They labeled it "Polluted Streams,"
> The body floating with the name.

The victims are ambiguous: sometimes they seem to be
identified with the poet, sometimes they are separate; this
coalescence and diffusion resembles the dream-work of
the mind. The helpless and crippled, the innocent and
kindly, are chief among these victims. In the midst of
this nightmare the poet undergoes with them their anguish and deprivation. Here, as elsewhere, Kunitz' position is something like that of a Christian without theology or supernatural faith whose sympathy and love
dictate an outraged dramatic speech. Toward the close of
the poem he too falls victim to the final stage of the surgeons' dissection:

> Lastly they squeezed out of my veins
> The bright liquor of sympathy;
> I lost the touch of souls, the reins
> On white revenge, and I was free
> Of pity, a solid man of snow.
> But in the night to whom could I go?

The crushing irony of these lines resides in the victim's fate: he is not killed but, worse, spiritually and emotionally maimed. In the encompassing darkness of the world that this poem evokes, human ties are severed and the person anaesthetized into a cipher of mute passions, frozen sensibilities, and ravaged intelligence. Kunitz' only answer, if it can be called as much, is a tiny wedge of hope and rebellion thrust between the closing doors of this monstrous world:

> Lie down with me, dear girl, before
> My butcher boys begin to rave.
> "No hope for persons any more,"
> They cry, "on either side of the grave."
> Tell them I say the heart forgives
> The world. Yes, I believe. In love.

Who is the girl? Her precise identity is not important. The first line of the stanza should be understood in part at least as metaphorical rather than completely literal, for sexuality as Kunitz uses it here covers the full range of feeling that exists in the communion of two individuals. The sexual act symbolizes any act of defiance toward the surgeons' decree that persons *as* persons are to be vanquished. And the last line of the stanza in effect echoes the first, supports it without equivocation or disguise. Nothing could prove more convincingly, I think, the humanizing element in Kunitz' poetry and his ability to employ it dramatically at the right moment to astonishing purpose.

Kunitz' early poems, as I have said, show a tendency to turn inward in the course of meditation. The mind itself is an enclosure or space for dramatic events: speakers and actors are introduced; imaginary scenes light up and disappear; biological investigations disclose the progress of corruption and decay in the human organism. A firm poetic intelligence probes these characters, situations, and images within its province in relentless quest of lasting answers and truths. The ultimate discoveries are usually tragic, but they inevitably throw Kunitz back on, and increase his awareness of, his own spiritual resources.

The later poetry changes this approach somewhat. While there is no lessening of intensity, Kunitz appears interested in moving his vision outside the arena of the mind. The result in many instances is an overt moral concern, a severe but compassionate dialogue with the world and its ways based on careful observation tempered by strong emotions. No doubt the growing political confusion and violence of the 1930s, culminating in World War II, distracted Kunitz from some of his previous artistic directions. "The Last Picnic," "Careless Love," "Night Letter," "Reflections by a Mailbox," "This Day This World," and "The Economist's Song" are among the best poems of this new type. Even when the poet now speaks of himself or takes himself and his art as the subject of a poem, there is in evidence a certain change of emphasis. Kunitz looks upon his vocation as a poet within a given time and place in history too. The closing lines of his poem "The Summing-Up" boldly define his later view: "I carve again on the lintel of the year/My sign: Mobility—and damn the cost!"

"Night Letter" presents Kunitz' new themes and outgoing tendencies in an arresting way. Like many of his poems it is composed in the form of a monologue, and the added epistolary technique of direct address involves the reader at once in the things described. The poet begins with himself, his failures and uncertainty; against personal dissatisfaction and a sense of guilt he puts the necessity of writing this letter (i.e., the poem). The recipient of the letter remains mysteriously obscure, though it is most likely the beloved woman whose guidance and understanding he needs. But the poem quickly passes beyond its initial mood of quiet nocturnal thought, and the poet is nearly overcome by the hallucinatory images that burst upon him when he requests her aid:

> Where is your ministry? I thought I heard
> A piece of laughter break upon the stair
> Like glass, but when I wheeled around I saw
> Disorder, in a tall magician's hat,
> Keeping his rabbit-madness crouched inside,
> Sit at my desk and scramble all the news.
> The strangest things are happening. Christ! the
>   dead,
> Pushing the membrane from their face, salute
> The dead and scribble slogans on our walls;
> Phantoms and phobias mobilize, thronging
> The roads; and in the Bitch's streets the men
> Are lying down, great crowds with fractured wills
> Dumping the shapeless burden of their lives
> Into the rivers where the motors flowed.

The once peaceful night has become a dark well issuing an apocalyptic imagery of public life which possesses the poet's mind. "Disorder" does less to "scramble all the news" than to expose in its grotesque, surreal details the underlying meanings and outcome of our modern civilization. Among Kunitz' contemporaries, Randall Jarrell, John Berryman, and Karl Shapiro have devised, in their own distinctive manners, patterns of irrational imagery to display the frightening dream of the public world. "Night Letter" makes a suitable companion-piece to "The Surgeons," but goes even further in specifying the infectious diseases of the spirit in the present age. Kunitz does not, however, simply halt with destructive images, ones which recall *The Dunciad* and *The Waste Land* in the severity of their judgment; in the next stanza certain ghosts, the tattered remnants of industrial society, its aims and methods, loom out of the shadows as Disorder continues to play his tricks:

Of those that stood in my doorway, self-accused,
Besmeared with failure in the swamps of trade,
One put a gun in his examiner's hand,
Making the judgment loud; another squats
Upon the asylum floor and plays with toys,
Like the spiral of a soul balanced on a stone,
Or a new gadget for slicing off the thumb;
The rest whirl in the torment of our time.
What have we done to them that what they are
Shrinks from the touch of what they hoped to be?

The air in which these lost, suicidal figures move about
and show themselves reminds us most of that bleak rushing wind of Dante's spirits of the Futile in the *Inferno*.
But the hell of Kunitz' poem is a hell of our own invention, wherein we lock ourselves with greed, exploitation,
and hatred of self and others. Is this not another picture
of the same living death that Joyce and Eliot and Lawrence, to choose obvious examples, have drawn for us
before? I make these allusions not to charge Kunitz with
a mere repetition of his elders' work—his poem is original and forceful—but to indicate the common ground
of the modern artistic conscience.

Though he denies many of the values and desires of
this society in the poem and vividly depicts their negative
effects, Kunitz realizes he cannot just shrug them off. He
must, instead, endure their deceit and baseness within
himself in order to chasten his poetic vision. Furthermore,
he refuses to accept any idea of a lasting human defeat.
Written in anguish and doubt, this poem, like his others,
still testifies to a love that binds persons together in true
community. The message of history Kunitz urges on us is
a recognition of this first and final potentiality of men
rising from the ashes of society or state. Beyond the general evil, he insists, that one value can be preserved:

I suffer the twentieth century,
The nerves of commerce wither in my arm;

Violence shakes my dreams, I am so cold,
Chilled by the persecuting wind abroad,
The oratory of the rodent's tooth,
The slaughter of the blue-eyed open towns,
And principle disgraced, and art denied.
My dear, is it too late for peace, too late
For men to gather at the wells to drink
The sweet water; too late for fellowship
And laughter at the forge; too late for us
To say, "Let us be good unto each other"?
The lamps go singly out; the valley sleeps;
I tend the last light shining on the farms
And keep for you the thought of love alive,
As scholars dungeoned in an ignorant age
Tended the embers of the Trojan fire.
Cities shall suffer siege and some shall fall,
But man's not taken. What the deep heart means,
Its message of the big, round, childish hand,
Its wonder, its simple lonely cry,
The bloodied envelope addressed to you,
Is history, that wide and mortal pang.

Kunitz lays the bulk of moral responsibility on the individual, and he speaks as an individual acutely conscious
of his own responsibilities. We can see just how conscious
he is if we notice the self-involvement in his poems, his
willing exposure there to the blows of experience; "I suffer the twentieth century" sums up Kunitz' imaginative
and moral effort. From inner conflicts and reflections as
well as from the larger external forces at war with man's
dignity and freedom, Kunitz has created a poetry that
talks to us by turns lyrically and savagely, and with disturbing honesty; his is a voice that has long needed to be
heard.

III

Theodore Roethke

Looking back to the early poetry of Theodore Roethke, whose premature death in August 1963 was an incalculable loss to American literature, we can see there the source of many of his constant thematic interests and of the restless exploratory impulse in technique that resulted from them. Roethke wished continually to plumb new areas of experience and to alter his style to match his discoveries. This impulse and his considerable lyric gifts give to the body of his writing a strong cumulative effect, for each successive stage of the work grows quite naturally from its predecessors. Reading his late poems, we feel the weight of earlier ones as an actual presence. By means of this closely woven pattern there is built up a universe of discourse, a poetic world of recurring themes and preoccupations into which the individual poems fit and within which they are comprehended.

Roethke's first book, *Open House* (1941), impresses the reader at the start with this poet's ability to sing, with his sharp, compact lines and his fundamental rhythmic sense. One is sure after seeing the best of these short lyrics and descriptive poems that Roethke could never have stopped with them; flexibility and the promise of

real development lurk everywhere under the surface of
his language and in the materials of his experience. In
the title poem he announces the major theme that will
influence nearly all of his future work and the artistic personality inseparable from it:

> My secrets cry aloud.
> I have no need for tongue.
> My heart keeps open house,
> My doors are widely swung.
> An epic of the eyes
> My love, with no disguise.
>
> My truths are all foreknown,
> This anguish self-revealed.
> I'm naked to the bone,
> With nakedness my shield.
> Myself is what I wear:
> I keep the spirit spare.
>
> The anger will endure,
> The deed will speak the truth
> In language strict and pure.
> I stop my lying mouth:
> Rage warps my clearest cry
> To witless agony.

The art proposed in these stanzas is peculiarly personal,
"naked to the bone," and, we might say, resembles a journal, kept with great pain, which traces the path of a sensitive mind from bondage to freedom. Such is the course
Roethke follows through a substantial part of his poetry.
It appears too that this interest in the self as poetic theme
evolves from a kind of curative effort by the poet—the
exorcism of a demon, T. S. Eliot would call it. A pro-
gressive movement that takes place in his writing falls
into stages ranging from the psychological to the visionary and mystical. This classification necessarily slights

some excellent light verse and children's poems that are peripheral to the poet's main purposes and so will not be discussed here. Roethke sets out upon a journey in his work, a research into the hidden corners of the psyche; through his labors he seeks to secure the liberation and integration of the self. The poet must relive his own personal history and once more find his way back into the world in order to discover himself and his ties with creation anew. The developing body of Roethke's poetry over the length of his career creates a record of the self's mutations, its final relationship to nature, and the expansion into love and illumination, its last, anagogical disposition.

The series of brief poems opening *The Lost Son* (1948), Roethke's second collection, serves as an introduction to longer and more radical pieces in the same book. Roethke has stressed the eye as the most important organ (see his "Prayer," from *Open House*); and it is an eye of microscopic powers trained on the minute, thriving vegetable and mineral realms of the earth that determines the character of sensibility here. These poems remind us somewhat of Rimbaud's *Illuminations* and Whitman's *Leaves of Grass*, not so much in subject matter or method as in their bold affront to our habitual forms of perception. We are forced to see things differently, or to reject the poetry altogether. We are urged to strip away those winding cloths of category and convention in which we bury our sense of life, and to regain a simplicity of vision, a belief in human possibility. Lying flat on the soil, as we appear to do while reading these poems, our eyes level with the ground, we begin again with the elements of the natural world. Our origins are linked by correspondences with those elements. If this procedure of close attention to budding plants and tiny creatures clashes with our pretensions to adult dignity, Roethke shows us in "Cuttings (Later)" that such observation has a surprising relevance to our own estate:

> This urge, wrestle, resurrection of dry sticks,
> Cut stems struggling to put down feet,
> What saint strained so much,
> Rose on such lopped limbs to new life?

Should we disclaim recognition of this struggle, we either have failed to admit to ourselves the truth or have not risen to meet life. Roethke always succeeds in putting before us the images of grace and defection.

As he often remarked in commenting upon his writing, Roethke spent his youth around the greenhouses in Michigan owned by his father and uncle, who had a large flower business, and he absorbed the atmosphere and the minutiae of plant life with an intensity of interest and a sympathy that transformed them into both literal facts and dominant metaphors of his poetry. Early influenced by his reading of Wordsworth, John Clare, and Whitman, and later by Léonie Adams, he quickly found poetic examples to spur his personal fascination with the details and processes of nature. There is a human lesson to be learned that starts with a humble attitude toward the lower orders of creation and the knowledge of our connections with them. True growth requires us to return along the way we came and to touch once more the roots from which we sprang:

> When sprouts break out,
> Slippery as fish,
> I quail, lean to beginnings, sheath-wet.

Such imagery identifies man with a process in the natural world and relates him to its stubborn fecundity. This assertion of existence is evident in a poem such as "Root Cellar," where

> Nothing would give up life:
> Even the dirt kept breathing a small breath.

The shorter poems of this period are generally devoted to what Roethke calls "the minimal." Their repeated themes and metaphors furnish a basis for more ambitious efforts and point to new departures. In a poem entitled "Transplanting" we watch young plants being set down in fresh soil and, as if through the lens of a camera equipped with a timing device, we see them unfurl and bloom:

Watching hands transplanting,
Turning and tamping,
Lifting the young plants with two fingers,
Sifting in a palm-full of fresh loam,—
One swift movement,—
Then plumping in the bunched roots,
A single twist of the thumbs, a tamping and
    turning,
All in one,
Quick on the wooden bench,
A shaking down while the stem stays straight,
Once, twice, and a faint third thump,—
Into the flat-box it goes,
Ready for the long days under the sloped glass:

The sun warming the fine loam,
The young horns winding and unwinding,
Creaking their thin spines,
The underleaves, the smallest buds
Breaking into nakedness,
The blossoms extending
Out into the sweet air,
The whole flower extending outward,
Stretching and reaching.

Roethke has realized how the same striving upward into life (suggested by the continuous movement of participles in the second stanza of this one-sentence poem) is an essential activity of the human spirit. His perception leads him to examine in a series of longer poems the relationships between the developing inner world of the self and the objects and forces of physical nature. What is merely a proposed analogy between psychic and natural processes in earlier poems approaches an identification of the two in work that follows.

The longer poems, which extend and deepen Roethke's previous concerns, finally appear as a full sequence in *The Waking* (1953). In a feat of imaginative re-creation and poetic skill he dramatizes, by means of a technique that sometimes seems close to the novelist's method of interior monologue, the borderline regions of the conscious and the preconscious in a child as he slowly, and often painfully, ascends from the mysterious center of his origins toward selfhood and a communion with the external cosmos. As the body grows the spirit grows with it, and the exchange between them, with the added consideration of lives and things outside which impose upon the forming self, creates the drama of these poems. Intimate attachments to the animal, vegetable, and mineral levels of creation are disclosed, and along with them, a tension in the child-protagonist between the desire for his whole existence and a contrary attraction for death and the inanimate. In order to embody the immediacy of this evolution of self in the poems, Roethke turns away from the stricter conventions of his previous work to looser and more eclectic forms suitable for rendering this complicated interior drama. The poems register the impression of sensations from without on a rapidly shifting psychic life until we sense a dialectical arrangement between them. Passages contain abrupt changes:

> Tell me, great lords of sting,
> Is it time to think?
> When I say things fond,

> I hear singing.
>> ("O Lull Me, Lull Me")

conflict and isolation:

> A worm has a mouth.
> Who keeps me last?
> Fish me out.
> Please.
>> ("Where Knock Is Open Wide")

and unexpected juxtapositions everywhere:

> Such music in a skin!
> A bird sings in the bush of your bones.
> Tufty, the water's loose.
> Bring me a finger. This dirt's lonesome for grass.
>> ("Give Way, Ye Gates")

In spite of the difficulties caused by such associative and prelogical techniques, some of which should disappear once the reader surrenders himself to the purpose and rhythm of the poet's undertaking, we still find the same precise diction and familiar musical ease that distinguish Roethke's art. If the poems lack the rational order we found in *Open House*, this lack must be attributed to the fluid reality the poet tries to capture here. The adjustments demanded of us are more extreme than before. Entering the child-protagonist's mind, we must adopt a literalness of apprehension and discard the adult's acquired skepticism—though we must not, on the other hand, forget the sophisticated craftsmanship in these poems. The world, from the new point of view Roethke provides, is transformed into a densely populated, because animistic, universe where normal distinctions of subject and object, consciousness and unconsciousness, will and instinct are abolished, and synesthesia is an accepted mode of perception. Perhaps the license for such a departure in poetry can best be explained by a remark

the poet made in a recent essay (*Poetry*, October 1960).
"We must permit poetry to extend consciousness,"
Roethke says, "as far, as deeply, as particularly as it can,
to recapture, in Stanley Kunitz' phrase, what it has lost
to some extent in prose. We must realize, I think, that
the writer in freer forms must have an even greater fidelity
to his subject matter than the poet who has the support
of form." Roethke, as a reading of his collected verse will
prove, has worked in both manners; many of his late
poems display his wish to experiment with "freer forms,"
as do the poems of the childhood sequence.

These poems are, then, composed on a rationale wholly
their own, a logic nearer that of the dream or some ellip-
sis of thought and sensation than the calculating intelligence. We can say of them, as T. S. Eliot says in the
preface to his translation of St.-John Perse's *Anabase*,
that "there is a logic of the imagination as well as a logic
of concepts." Individually, the poems constitute portions
of a journey into the psyche, the memories and experiences beneath everyday conscious thought, and so they
participate in different temporal dimensions by disturbing the dormant past within the self. Roethke's poetic
enterprise at this juncture involves him in something resembling the interpretation of the many layers of writing
on a palimpsest; each one draws him further back in time
and into more obscure circumstances. But the journey is
made with direction and, we feel, even with urgency. It
is an attempt to win a perspective on the general plan of
personal existence from its remote beginnings by finding
the "lost son" and recovering the moments of that life
already lived. Only a simple-minded view would discount
these poems as clinical materials or the raw stuff of psychoanalysis; they are nothing of the sort. However private
the resources on which Roethke has called, the problem
of understanding details of separate poems seldom comes
from faults of privacy. The problem may be our own
carelessness or impatience. A statement Roethke wrote

for *Twentieth Century Authors* helps to clarify his intentions:

> I have tried to transmute and purify my "life," the sense of being defiled by it, in both small and formal and somewhat blunt short poems, and latterly, in longer poems which try in their rhythms to catch the very movement of the mind itself, to trace the spiritual history of a protagonist (not "I," personally), of all haunted and harried men; to make in this series . . . a true and not arbitrary order which will permit many ranges of feeling, including humor.

The universal character of Roethke's protagonist compels our participation in these inner travels. By association we are turned into partial actors of the drama his poems relate.

The journey back into childhood exposes old sores; and anxiety over questions about death, God, isolation, sexuality, and parental bonds looms large in the sequence. A desire to get out of the morass of such disturbances is the most pronounced feature of the protagonist, but he can attain his release only by facing directly all the hazards and powers—usually psychic ones—that endanger the gradually developing self. "The Lost Son" is probably the most representative poem of the group for our purposes because it holds within its careful design the prominent themes of the other poems and so forms a paradigm of the interior journey. The plan of the poem falls into several sections tracing the narrator/protagonist's progress: the setting forth, the quest (with its accompanying ordeals), the discovery of a new harmony and integrity, the protagonist's expectation of another phase, and his speculation on what has occurred.

"The Lost Son" follows the trials and decided advance of the self or, to use a Jungian term, charts a process of individuation. Beginning, ominously enough, with suggestions of death, gloom, and ugliness, the poem drops us into the middle of the child-protagonist's pursuit of freedom and singular identity, a pursuit frustrated by the shocks experience continues to administer to the frail equilibrium of his psychic life:

> At Woodlawn I heard the dead cry:
> I was lulled by the slamming of iron,
> A slow drip over stones,
> Toads brooding in wells.

The proximity of destruction and the riddle of his own nature lure the protagonist into action, and he engages himself in the search for liberation:

> Which is the way I take;
> Out of what door do I go,
> Where and to whom?

But confusion dogs his tracks, for the animistic universe where each thing has an independent and ambiguous character is nothing if not deceptive; like the magical forests of fairy tales it presents more false leads than true paths. The creatures, plants, and other entities filling this world, even the friendliest ones, haunt him, and yet he must inquire of them the way out. He looks among the smallest creatures for some reliable guides, though not always with happy results:

> All the leaves stuck out their tongues;
> I shook the softening chalk of my bones,
> Saying, Snail, snail, glister me forward,
> Bird, soft-sigh me home.

Under prevailing conditions movement offers the sole relief to the agonized protagonist, who is also heir to complaints of the flesh. His search brings him at last to "the pit," in the section of that title, and there he reaches the lowest and most dangerous point in the journey. In fact, the pit—clearly a female symbol—signifies the womb or place of his origins, and return to it indicates the risk of defeat, even of death. As the protagonist nears there to ask a fundamental question about life—"Who stunned the dirt into noise?"—he is answered with images of the womb and birth, "the slime of a wet nest." A harsh music of warning jangles his nerves, accompanied in section three, "The Gibber," by further alienation from his surroundings, sexual dilemmas, and shrill discord:

> Dogs of the groin
> Barked and howled,
> The sun was against me,
> The moon would not have me.
>
> The weeds whined,
> The snakes cried,
> The cows and briars
> Said to me: Die.

At the edge of annihilation the protagonist passes through the "storm's heart" and glides beyond it into a state of calm, another plane of being. The self, having survived the threats to its growth, breaks forth in a mood of spiritual exultation at the sheer pleasure of its attainment:

> These sweeps of light undo me.
> Look, look, the ditch is running white!
> I've more veins than a tree!
> Kiss me, ashes, I'm falling through a dark swirl.

Body and spirit revel in their newly won harmony. The freed self, no longer desperately struggling for independence, dissolves its conflicts with the physical world and, indeed, brings the things of that world into communion with it. The greenhouse, with its rich store of life, to which the young protagonist comes home after the quest within himself, becomes a scene of revelation and symbolizes both the unity and the potentiality of existence. This regenerative cycle is caught in the images of flowers:

> The rose, the chrysanthemum turned toward the
>   light.
> Even the hushed forms, the bent yellowy weeds
> Moved in a slow up-sway.

In the poem's last section the protagonist meditates on his experience. This is "an in-between time" when he can merely await further motions of the spirit. The imagery of the passage recalls T. S. Eliot's "Ash Wednesday" and *Four Quartets*, and the resemblance is doubtless intentional, as it is also in the later "Meditations of an Old Woman." But Eliot's poems treat spiritual development as the product of individual effort in prayer and contemplation and faith, whereas Roethke sees it as the outcome of a *natural* process. The latter's religious vision is intuitive and remains far from orthodox Christianity. The narrator of "The Lost Son" hesitates to classify his experience; he will admit of no more than a strange visitation:

> Was it light?
> Was it light within?
> Was it light within light?
> Stillness becoming alive,
> Yet still?

The allusion to Eliot's "still point of the turning world" may be obvious, but the meaning in Roethke's poem should prevent us from taking it as a literal echo. Whatever generates the spiritual odyssey in "The Lost Son" derives from within the protagonist himself and is not based upon a definite external creed:

> A lively understandable spirit
> Once entertained you.

> It will come again.
> Be still
> Wait.

That spirit does "come again" in Roethke's writings. Though he will long be occupied with the progress of the self, the conclusion of this poetic sequence enables him to proceed in different directions.

Roethke's love poems, which began to appear in *The Waking* and have their own section in *Words for the Wind* (1958), manifest certain sharp deviations from earlier self-examination. The amatory verse blends considerations of self with qualities of eroticism and sensuality; but more importantly, the poems introduce and maintain a fascination with something beyond the self, that is, with the figure of the other, or the beloved woman.

The beloved woman of these poems takes various forms. Sometimes she assumes the figure of a wraith, an entrancing specter; sometimes she is purely physical. Her role in the poems can be called that of the female principle or the opposite or the other and frequently involves metamorphosis. Observation of her beauties by the poet leads him to rapport with creation:

> The breath of a long root,
> The shy perimeter
> Of the unfolding rose,
> The green, the altered leaf,
> The oyster's weeping foot,
> And the incipient star—
> Are part of what she is.
> She wakes the ends of life.
> ("Words for the Wind")

In some way this loved one possesses the elusive secrets of life and its potentialities; she partakes of all that is. The style of the love poems returns to a more formal order after the experimentation of the sequence pieces, but Roethke has obviously learned a new disciplined richness of language and music from that venture.

Fulfillment in love is the theme of a quartet of lyrics, "Four for Sir John Davies," which extends the search for unity and harmony so visible in "The Lost Son" from an internal, psychological probing to a vision of the relationship between the self and the beloved. Drawing its basic metaphor of dancing from Davies' sixteenth-century poem *Orchestra*, which explains the hierarchical plan of the universe through that figure, and from Yeats, who saw in the dance an image of sexual and spiritual reconciliation, the poem leaves the poet's isolated dance at the beginning to discover a transcendent completion in which both lover and beloved share. At the start the poet celebrates the vital energies of the cosmos and of his own rhythmic movements, but the latter are occasionally humorous and lack agility and purpose:

> I tried to fling my shadow at the moon,
> The while my blood leaped with a wordless song.
> Though dancing needs a master, I had none
> To teach my toes to listen to my tongue.

In spite of the pleasures of his single dance, which gives him the feeling of kinship with *things*, the poet seeks a deeper human bond. Attraction to his newly found partner begins between "animal and human heat," but we soon realize that the meeting of the lovers physically has created a corresponding spiritual engagement:

> Incomprehensible gaiety and dread
> Attended all we did. Behind, before,
> Lay all the lonely pastures of the dead;
> The spirit and the flesh cried out for more.
> We two, together, on a darkening day
> Took arms against our own obscurity.

As traditionally befits such lovers, they receive, in the poem's third part, one identity. They recall that pair in Donne's "The Canonization" whose pure devotion to one another divorces them from the profane public world and invests them with a sacred or mystical quality, for here also, Roethke writes, "the flesh can make the spirit visible." So this dance, though it originates in human love, is anything but simply ordinary and mundane. The vertical motion of these dancers and the successive alterations they undergo in their ascent establish something close to a religious dimension in this experience. We cannot fail to see how love at its most intense, which the poems portray, is described by the poet as a spiritual event of such magnitude and significance that the lovers' connection with the universe is completely revised. In "The Vigil," the concluding poem, Dante's paradisaical vision is introduced to set off Roethke's own version of an encounter with the eternal; but this moment seems, as it did in "The Lost Son," a condition of inner blessedness the cause of which—outside of human love—is not fully known. Yet there is no doubt that the moment is one of visionary perception rendering creation, as it were, transparent and mysteriously transfiguring the couple:

> The world is for the living. Who are they?
> We dared the dark to reach the white and warm.
> She was the wind when wind was in my way;
> Alive at noon, I perished in her form.
> Who rise from flesh to spirit know the fall:
> The word outleaps the world, and light is all.

Roethke dedicates himself much of the time, particularly in his later work, to the accomplishment of poetic moments such as the one above, and in his *Sequence, Sometimes Metaphysical* (1963) openly searches for God in poems clearly written from a firsthand knowledge of the soul's dark night. But neither the ecstatic assertions

of being nor the often tormented mystical visions hide
from Roethke the realities of human life, indeed they
are seen as the expression of that life at its zenith, when
the self reaches in every direction to the heart of things.
The concluding "Meditations of an Old Woman" from
Words for the Wind, the visionary pieces of Sequence,
Sometimes Metaphysical, and many other poems that
have been published in various journals and are collected
in The Far Field (1964) amply demonstrate the poet's
repeated realization of these moments and his contemplation of the extremes of mortal experience.

"Meditations of an Old Woman," the group of five
poems at the end of Words for the Wind, is a noteworthy
achievement looking toward more recent experiments
with a long, prose-style line in "Meditation at Oyster
River," "The Rose," and other poems. Composed freely,
the "Meditations" are sometimes said to be derivative
from Four Quartets, but actually they owe, as Roethke
confirmed, a larger debt to Whitman in both style and
attitude, a debt that becomes even more plain in work
that follows. Yet a limited confusion is understandable
when we acknowledge that the poems are to a degree an
answer to Eliot's mature view. The old woman who is the
speaker of these reflective monologues serves as an opposite to Eliot, whose voice we hear throughout Four Quartets; and the conclusions at which she arrives in the
course of the meditations about herself and the meaning
of her existence have little in common with Eliot's. In
fact, some passages like the following from "What Can I
Tell My Bones?" can only be read as a direct reply to
him—with slight overtones of parody:

> It is difficult to say all things are well,
> When the worst is about to arrive;
> It is fatal to woo yourself,
> However graceful the posture.

Loved heart, what can I say?
When I was a lark, I sang;
When I was a worm, I devoured.

The self says, I am;
The heart says, I am less;
The spirit says, you are nothing.

Old age, a retrospective look at life, and the approach of death are themes of both Roethke's and Eliot's poems, though their final visions diverge widely. In contrast to the prayer and asceticism and renunciation of the world on which *Four Quartets* is founded Roethke's elderly lady embraces in memory and imagination the entire spectrum of her experience, its joys and delights, its sufferings and disappointments included. These meditations at last do more than just affirm the precious unevenness of life; they celebrate with religious exaltation its multitude of beauties and the horizons of possibility in evidence even at its close.

While the narrator of the poems was inspired by Roethke's mother, she is a mask for the poet too. The poems move with the changes of her thought, touching on incidents and ideas of a long lifetime that revolve in her mind with many of Roethke's favorite images and metaphors from the natural world: the sun, the wind, the tiny creatures of earth, flowers and seeds and grass, water, and so on. But the poems turn to other matters as well; there is a brilliant and savage passage on modern forms of self-destruction in women, which leads also to suffering or destruction in those about them:

I think of the self-involved:
The ritualists of the mirror, the lonely drinkers,
The minions of benzedrine and paraldehyde,
And those who submerge themselves deliberately
    in trivia,

Women who become their possessions,
Shapes stiffening into metal,
Match-makers, arrangers of picnics—
What do their lives mean,
And the lives of their children?——
The young, brow-beaten early into a baleful
    silence,
Frozen by a father's lip, a mother's failure to
    answer.
Have they seen, ever, the sharp bones of the
    poor?
Or known, once, the soul's authentic hunger,
Those cat-like immaculate creatures
For whom the world works?

These lines expose graphically the failure of the self to rise toward completion, a warping and perversion that contrast with the stalwart openness to surrounding reality so noticeable in the old woman. Though she is not always serene and knows fear, hesitation, and loneliness at certain times, the narrator can declare, in the last two stanzas of the final poem, her faith in the durable splendor of the world and in the miraculous transformation or rebirth the spirit works in the individual:

The sun! The sun! And all we can become!
And the time ripe for running to the moon!
In the long fields, I leave my father's eye;
And shake the secrets from my deepest bones;
My spirit rises with the rising wind;
I'm thick with leaves and tender as a dove,
I take the liberties a short life permits—
I seek my own meekness;
I recover my tenderness by long looking.
By midnight I love everything alive.
Who took the darkness from the air?

I'm wet with another life.
Yea, I have gone and stayed.

What came to me vaguely is now clear,
As if released by a spirit,
Or agency outside me.
Unprayed-for,
And final.

Though Roethke again chooses to keep his ultimate
view somewhat indefinite, his later poetry has in general
become more religious and mystical. In other poems
from *Words for the Wind*, as well as in his last writings,
he addresses himself solely to the presentation of his
visionary experience. Some of these poems focus on the
negative aspects of this experience, on the dilemmas in
which the self is trapped, on psychic and spiritual torments, in a style that is musical but also terse and epi-
grammatic, with rapidly changing imagery. Roethke's
concerns have progressed from those of the earlier childhood sequence poems, but we can still observe his extremely moving evocations of irrational, dreamlike perception. "The Exorcism" is a poem of spiritual pursuit
and of the agony of purification that is the necessary
preparation for experience or knowledge of the Divine.
The poet is brought face to face with his soul's imperfections and must undergo the pain of being parted from
them:

1
The gray sheep came. I ran,
My body half in flame.
(Father of flowers, who
Dares face the thing he is?)

As if pure being woke,
The dust rose and spoke;

A shape cried from a cloud,
Cried to my flesh out loud.

(And yet I was not there,
But down long corridors,
My own, my secret lips
Babbling in urinals.)

2
In a dark wood I saw—
I saw my several selves
Come running from the leaves,
Lewd, tiny, careless lives
That scuttled under stones,
Or broke, but would not go.
I turned upon my spine,
I turned and turned again,
A cold God-furious man
Writhing until the last
Forms of his secret life
Lay with the dross of death.

I was myself, alone.

I broke from that low place
Breathing a slower breath,
Cold, in my own dead salt.

Two lines from another poem, "Elegy," might serve
as a helpful gloss on the theme of "The Exorcism":

I have myself, and bear its weight of woe
That God that God leans down His heart to hear.

Yet "The Exorcism" and "Elegy" show us only the
darker side of Roethke's religious imagination, which is
more than counterbalanced by his positive insight, the
gift of a sudden and joyful revelation:

Dry bones! Dry bones! I find my loving heart,
Illumination brought to such a pitch
I see the rubblestones begin to stretch
As if reality had split apart
And the whole motion of the soul lay bare:
I find that love, and I am everywhere.
(*"The Renewal"*)

Here the poet, at the peak of vision, feels himself entering into the very essence of created things: knower and known are no longer separated by barriers of physical solidity or by appearances. The ordinary rubblestones that break open and disclose their hidden being to the poet do so only as he sees himself in the same undisguised way. Extraordinary as such a revelation is, and it is merely one of a number, we find, especially in some of Roethke's newest and most unusual poems, a profound sense of communion with this reality, though it is set forth in a more relaxed and detailed manner. These poems are freed of regular meters, and use long lines and an approach to reality previously seen in the "Meditations of an Old Woman." Roethke says (*Poetry*, October 1960); "There are areas of experience in modern life that simply cannot be rendered by either the formal lyric or straight prose. We need the catalogue in our time. We need the eye close on the object, and the poem about the single incident—the animal, the child." That is precisely what we get from Roethke—"the catalogue," "the eye close on the object"—in "Meditation at Oyster River," "Journey to the Interior," "The Rose," "The Long Waters," and other poems. He has named for us, one way or another, his predecessors in this mode as he went along; they are Christopher Smart, Walt Whitman, and D. H. Lawrence. To catch the feeling of this sort of poem, so rare in modern literature, we have to read more than two or three lines; here, then, are sections four and five of "The Long Waters":

IV

In the vaporous gray of early morning,
Over the thin, feathery ripples breaking lightly
    against the irregular shoreline—
Feathers of the long swell, burnished, almost
    oily—
A single wave comes in like the neck of a great
    swan
Swimming slowly, its back ruffled by the light
    cross-winds,
To a tree lying flat, its crown half broken.

I remember a stone breaking the eddying current,
Neither white nor red, in the dead middle way,
Where impulse no longer dictates, nor the dark-
    ening shadow,
A vulnerable place,
Surrounded by sand, broken shells, the wreckage
    of water.

V

As light reflects from a lake, in late evening,
When bats fly, close to slightly tilting brownish
    water,
And the low ripples run over a pebbly shoreline,
As a fire, seemingly long dead, flares up from a
    downdraft of air in a chimney,
Or the breeze moves over the knees from a low
    hill,
So the sea wind wakes desire.
My body shimmers with a light flame.

I see in the advancing and retreating waters
The shape that came from my sleep, weeping:
The eternal one, the child, the swaying vine
    branch,
The numinous ring around the opening flower,

The friend that runs before me on the windy
    headlands,
Neither voice nor vision.

I, who came back from the depths laughing too
    loudly,
Become another thing;
My eyes extend beyond the farthest bloom of the
    waves;
I lose and find myself in the long waters;
I am gathered together once more;
I embrace the world.

This poem, like the other "catalogue" poems of this
last phase of Roethke's work, enumerates objects and details of the world fondly remembered and treasured as
parts of the poet's spiritual odyssey. Thus the contemplation of external details in the universe never takes complete precedence over the consciousness of the poet; a
relationship always exists between what has been seen in
nature and the interior state of the observer. It seems clear
from the end of "The Long Waters" that Roethke experiences a cycle of dispersal and reunification somewhat
similar to the pattern in "The Exorcism" or "The Renewal," though the "embrace" of the final line here does
not come with a blinding flash of mystical intuition but
rather as a condition of the poet's soul gradually reached
through the entire slow movement of the poem.

"The Long Waters" and the visionary lyrics of *Sequence, Sometimes Metaphysical* exemplify the last stage
in the long metamorphosis of the self that Roethke attained in his poetry. This fundamental theme gave his
work unity and yet never restricted the astonishing variety, invention, and artistry of which he was capable.
Other modern poets have taken the self as theme, but no
one has so fruitfully sounded his own subjective depths.
Nor have any of his contemporaries been granted such

an intimate communion with nature. (Eberhart grows ecstatic over the mystical suggestiveness of natural things on occasion, but he does not penetrate so deeply into it as Roethke, and he does not have the latter's vision of a profound evolutionary pattern.) Roethke's uncanny sensibilities led him to comprehend and to incorporate in his writing the continuous but nearly imperceptible communication that goes on among all living things, as well as to know moments of heightened awareness in which his relation and that of the created world to the Divine were suggested. He once said (in *New World Writing* 4) that the poet "may be lucky enough, on occasion, to create a complete reality in a single poem." Few poets of modern times have known this luck as often as Theodore Roethke.

Elizabeth Bishop

Elizabeth Bishop is one of those poets of rare sensitivity, meticulous craftsmanship, and limited production whose work is of such a high caliber that she must be set apart from many of her more prolific rivals. Miss Bishop has, so far, published only two collections of verse, with a third one recently announced but not yet published at the time of this writing. In 1955 she combined a new group of poems with her first volume, *North and South* (1946), and made what her publishers call a collected edition under the title *Poems: North and South & A Cold Spring*. Miss Bishop more than compensates for her limited canon by her impeccable artistic judgment; even the slightest piece of her work is finished to perfection, glows with an unchangeable completeness. The poetic universe created within this framework of formal excellence, a universe translated by language into something unmistakably hers, as if she had dreamed it up just for her own contemplation, stands out with marvelous fullness and with an admirable exactitude:

> Each barge on the river easily tows
>   a mighty wake,

a giant oak-leaf of gray lights
    on duller gray;
and behind it real leaves are floating by,
    down to the sea.
Mercury-veins on the giant leaves,
    the ripples, make
for the sides of the quai, to extinguish themselves
    against the walls
as softly as falling stars come to their ends
    at a point in the sky.
And throngs of small leaves, real leaves, trailing
    them, go drifting by
to disappear as modestly, down the seas'
    dissolving halls.
We stand as still as stones to watch
    the leaves and ripples
while light and nervous water hold
    their interview.
"If what we see could forget us half as easily,"
    I want to tell you,
"as it does itself—but for life we'll not be rid
    of the leaves' fossils."

                  ("Quai d'Orleans")

This beautifully done poem represents the more ambitious side of Miss Bishop's efforts, which is also the
side of her greatest successes. The ambitious attempt I
wish to suggest in these poems is less a matter of achievement in strictly formal terms—an achievement we might
just as well grant Elizabeth Bishop to begin with—than
it is a matter of the perception of reality, which is the
total accomplishment of language, technique, music,
and imagery working simultaneously, or "the complete
consort dancing together" of T. S. Eliot's "Little Gid-
ding." In this category we find "The Imaginary Iceberg,"
"The Man-Moth," "A Miracle for Breakfast," "The
Weed," "The Monument," "Florida," "Roosters," "The

Fish," "Over 2000 Illustrations and a Complete Con
cordance," "Invitation to Miss Marianne Moore," and
"Insomnia." Of course, this list grows out of my per
sonal preferences; other readers will have their own. But
I believe most lists will include a good number of these
poems. In the minor or lighter, which is to say, less am
bitious, poems Miss Bishop contents herself—delight
fully, to be sure—with the surface of things, with sheer
elegance and grace and play of wit; she refrains from
directing all her imaginative strength toward deeper in
volvement and complex revelation. "Sleeping on the
Ceiling," "The Colder the Air," "Wading at Wellfleet,"
"Chemin de Fer," "Argument," and "From the Country
to the City" are all good examples of this second group
of poems. The last of them, for instance, uses a bright
and fanciful conceit to link highway and landscape in
the recumbent figure of a clown. This opening passage
sufficiently conveys the general effect:

> The long, long legs,
> league-boots of land, that carry the city nowhere,
>   nowhere; the lines
> that we drive on (satin-stripes on harlequin's
>   trousers, tights);
> his tough trunk dressed in tatters, scribbled over
>   with nonsensical signs;
> his shadowy, tall dunce-cap; and, best of all his
>   shows and sights,
> his brain appears, throned in "fantastic triumph,"
>   and shines through his hat
> with jeweled works at work at intermeshing
>   crowns, lamé with lights.

Miss Bishop's inventiveness in this poem is truly remarkable, and it is sustained through each skillful line
to the end. Yet the ingredients of fantasy and morality
are not put to the service of as penetrating a view as

they are elsewhere. This judgment should be taken as a distinction, not a condemnation.

"Quai d'Orleans" may be seen as a useful introductory poem to Miss Bishop's work because it exhibits so clearly three dominant elements to be found in one degree or another in her poetry, though not always together. The first of these elements, the most immediately recognizable as well as the most ubiquitous, is accuracy of descriptive detail. Miss Bishop everywhere indulges herself, to the reader's pleasure, in the particularity of things, in their quality, multiplicity, and variousness. Robert Lowell has compared her to Russian novelists, rather than to other poets, in this respect; and Randall Jarrell states in *Poetry and the Age* that "all her poems have written underneath, *I have seen it.*" That seeing, which contributes to, but is not completely identical with, the perception of reality already noted in connection with the best of Miss Bishop's poems, is evident in "Quai d'Orleans," where it functions in two interdependent and inseparable ways. One consists quite plainly of the pure act of visual apprehension:

> And throngs of small leaves, real leaves, trailing
>   them, go drifting by. . . .

More substantial passages of straight description are located in different poems:

> Enormous turtles, helpless and mild,
> die and leave their barnacled shells on the beaches,
> and their large white skulls with round eye-sockets
> twice the size of a man's.
>
> ("Florida")

> The big fish tubs are completely lined
> with layers of beautiful herring scales
> and the wheelbarrows are similarly plastered

with creamy iridescent coats of mail,
with small iridescent flies crawling on them.
("At the Fishhouses")

Such exquisite presentation of the world of physical
fact is itself rich in human meanings and may well remind us of the Chilean poet Pablo Neruda's insistence
that poets "look closely at the world of objects at rest."
Neruda continues: "In them one sees the confused im-
purity of the human condition, the massing of things,
the use and disuse of substances, footprints and finger-
prints, the abiding presence of the human engulfing all
artifacts, inside and out" (from *Selected Poems of Pablo
Neruda*, translated by Ben Belitt). But if we start search-
ing for these passages we will soon notice how difficult
it is to find those that are merely unalloyed descriptions,
that is, descriptions not further enriched or transmuted by
metaphor and simile. Even the lines quoted above from
"At the Fishhouses" have their metaphorical content in
"coats of mail." A second kind of seeing, then, is the act
of visual apprehension complicated, extended, deepened,
or whatever, by metaphor; and it is this type that provides most of what we see in "Quai d'Orleans." Description without metaphor or simile may set up resonances
or vibrations that we can feel inwardly but cannot put
our fingers on, whereas metaphor itself boldly adds to
things already there by suggesting new patterns of relation and including them as part of what is actually present. Thus the barge's wake on the river at the beginning
of the poem is perceived at once as something else, "a
giant oak-leaf of gray lights/on duller gray," which helps
to produce the haunting autumnal atmosphere of the
scene holding the observer's attention. "The seas'/dis-
solving halls" is another metaphorical phrase increasing
the dominant mood of fatality, loss, and dissolution in
the poem.

The next prominent element in "Quai d'Orleans" that

reflects Miss Bishop's general practice is a metaphorical
extension of described things which permits those things
to give birth to a reality somehow different from our
known one, a reality that we accept nonetheless because
it operates smoothly and naturally according to its own
laws of "pure imagination," in Coleridge's phrase. I
mean, of course, the element of fantasy. The element is
not so strong in this as in other poems—"The Man-
Moth" or "A Miracle for Breakfast," for instance—but
its makings are obvious enough in the developing metaphor of the "giant oak-leaf" of the barge's wake, mentioned before, which passes beyond consideration as a
descriptive device, intensifying the scene to become
finally the reality contemplated:

> Mercury-veins on the giant leaves,
>   the ripples, make
> for the sides of the quai, to extinguish themselves
>   against the walls
> as softly as falling-stars come to their ends
>   at a point in the sky.

The observer/poet, and the reader with her, is caught
up in a world of imagery which began in fact and now
keeps enlarging itself. But the extinguishing of the "fall-
ing-stars," toward which the leaves that are really ripples
tend, returns the observer to actuality, for the next line
again concentrates on the factual rather than the metaphorical leaves—"real leaves," Miss Bishop calls them to
remind us of her return—"drifting by" on the waters.
The excursion into fantasy in this poem is very limited,
though, when compared with some of the author's other
pieces in which it rules throughout.

Accomplished and acceptable fantasy is a distinguishing feature of Miss Bishop's poetry and one that certainly calls upon all of her powers. Her enterprise in this
mode is even more amazing when we stop to think how
modern poets have usually been much less interested in

fantasy than writers of prose fiction. Yet a poem like
"The Man-Moth," the title of which derives from a
"newspaper misprint for 'mammoth'" the poet once
read, gains memorable and terrifying effects reminiscent
of Kafka, or Borges in his fables. Point of view fashions
an eerie, distorted universe from a nighttime metropolis
overlooked by the distant and enigmatic face of the
moon, which governs with shadow, dream, illusion, and
unreason when the logic of day vanishes into darkness.
When we read "The Man-Moth," we should recall that
Jules Laforgue, T. S. Eliot, Wallace Stevens, and other
moderns use the moon's appearance as such a symbol, as
well as one for the imagination:

> Here, above,
> cracks in the buildings are filled with battered
>   moonlight.
> The whole shadow of Man is only as big as his hat.
> It lies at his feet like a circle for a doll to stand on,
> and he makes an inverted pin, the point magnet-
>   ized to the moon.
> He does not see the moon; he observes only her
>   vast properties,
> feeling the queer light on his hands, neither warm
>   nor cold,
> of a temperature impossible to record in ther-
>   mometers.

If this is man's world at night, it still looks quite different to the Man-Moth, a desolate, fantastic creature
who is without a doubt more human in his curious way
than anything else in the poem. "He emerges/from an
opening under the edge of one of the sidewalks," and
even more like a moth, he tries to ascend toward the
source of light, the moon. Though he climbs by instinct
or unquestioned impulse, thoughts and feelings of a kind
we would normally consider it improbable to associate
with a moth are attributed to him—and not only here

out throughout the rest of the poem. The Man-Moth 'thinks the moon is a small hole at the top of the sky," and he thinks that, fearful as he is of this expedition, he might enter it "and be forced through, as from a tube, in black scrolls on the light." We are left to determine for ourselves whether success would mean escape into another universe or annihilation or what, but we cannot pause for long to decide because

> . . . . what the Man-Moth fears most he must
>   do, although
> he fails, of course, and falls back scared but quite
>   unhurt.

His attempted ascent is followed by descent, the return to his habitation, which leads the poem further into regions of darkness. The Man-Moth works his way back "to the pale subways of cement he calls his home"; but these are no longer the mere cracks of sidewalks or building walls seen earlier for they become, as in a dream, actual subways:

>   He flits,
> he flutters, and cannot get aboard the silent trains
> fast enough to suit him. The doors close swiftly.
> The Man-Moth always seats himself facing the
>   wrong way
> and the train starts at once at its full, terrible
>   speed,
> without a shift in gears or a gradation of any sort.
> He cannot tell the rate at which he travels back-
>   wards.
>
>   Each night he must
> be carried through artificial tunnels and dream
>   recurrent dreams.
> Just as the ties recur beneath the train, these
>   underlie

his rushing brain. He does not dare look out the
   window,
for the third rail, the unbroken draught of poison,
runs there beside him. He regards it as a disease
he has inherited the susceptibility to. He has to
   keep
his hands in his pockets, as others must wear
   mufflers.

Though these lines are occasionally tinged with wit
and irony, the general picture is somber and, I should
say, nearly infernal. This effect is emphasized by the general "flatness" of the poem's music. The subway imagery
calls to mind those sections of T. S. Eliot's *Four Quartets* which have as their setting the black tunnels of the
London underground, and they, in their turn, recall
Dante's Hell in *The Divine Comedy*. But the details of
his habits and terrors, his private rituals aboard the train,
link the Man-Moth with Kafka's characters and Henri
Michaux's victimized figure Plume. The inevitability of
all he does, his climb, failure, and descent into hellish,
or at least purgatorial, regions of the subway, supplies
the poem with its most frightening aspect. Fantasy
makes that aspect credible, for once we enter the world
of the poem we must assume its laws as a matter of
course.

The concluding stanza brings us close to the Man-
Moth, elicits our sympathy, and confirms our sense of
the poem as a kind of parable of human existence. Yet
the self-sufficient reality of the fantasy world is not vio-
lated; it is strengthened by the intimate approach to the
Man-Moth himself. The relationship between his world
and ours takes form in the tear we may receive ("pure
enough to drink") from the center of his life, as it were
—a life fertile with experiences we should acknowledge.
In the Man-Moth's tear there exists the possibility of
communion:

                           If you catch him,
hold up a flashlight to his eye. It's all dark pupil,
an entire night itself, whose haired horizon
      tightens
as he stares back, and closes up the eye. Then from
      the lids
one tear, his only possession, like the bee's sting,
      slips.
Slyly he palms it, and if you're not paying
      attention
he'll swallow it. However, if you watch, he'll hand
      it over,
cool as from underground springs and pure
      enough to drink.

Moral vision, the interpretation and judgment of experience, constitutes the third and last element of Miss
Bishop's poetry I want to emphasize in these few pages.
Frequently this vision, which springs from the poet's
search for truth at the heart of her creation—in fact, *is*
that truth—occurs as the final portion of a poem. Quite
evidently this is the case in "The Man-Moth," where
the capture of this sad, strange creature is charged with
the potentialities of a new and different relationship, one
that will issue, correspondingly, in a new and different
understanding on the captor's part. In "Quai d'Orleans"
the element of moral vision can be separated readily from
the remainder of the poem; it is isolated as a separate
quoted comment, a concluding spoken observation that
draws its meaning and value from the vivid experience
in the preceding lines. The meaning and value are not
allegorical with reference to the details of experience the
poem utilizes; rather, they indicate the possible significance implicit in the experience considered as a whole.
In other words, the poet generalizes, with a peculiarly
prophetic note struck in her last words ("but for life
we'll not be rid/of the leaves' fossils"), from the scene

she has been watching and meditating upon, though she keeps her generalization linked to the specific by using "leaves' fossils" both as a term of her concluding thought or moral vision and as a recollection of the experience on which she bases it.

Elizabeth Bishop's interest in judgment as the knot tying a poem together relates her, as critics have pointed out, to Marianne Moore, whom she sometimes resembles stylistically, notably in her love of the particular. But if Miss Bishop has her occasional literary debts, she still shows up much more strongly on the credit side of originality and singularity of mind and poetic approach than she does on the side of influence and indebtedness. She is certainly her own poet.

Beyond her moral vision—lest we take her for a grave moralizer, which she is not—there is her love for and permanent delight in the realm of appearances, in all that she comes in contact with in day-to-day reality. There are artistic moments, such as we discover in her marvelous "Invitation to Miss Marianne Moore," when that love is inspired by a joyous vein of fantasy:

> From Brooklyn, over the Brooklyn Bridge, on this
>   fine morning,
>   please come flying.
> In a cloud of fiery pale chemicals,
>   please come flying,
> to the rapid rolling of thousands of small blue
>   drums
> descending out of the mackerel sky
> over the glittering grandstand of harbor-water,
>   please come flying.
>
> Whistles, pennants and smoke are blowing. The
>   ships
> are signaling cordially with multitudes of flags
> rising and falling like birds all over the harbor.

Enter: two rivers, gracefully bearing
countless little pellucid jellies
in cut-glass epergnes dragging with silver chains.
The flight is safe; the weather is all arranged.
The waves are running in verses this fine morning.
    Please come flying.

These stanzas really bring us full circle in Miss Bishop's
work, for we are where we began, in the world so closely
perceived by the poet's eye. While she always treats
creation as though it were a chest of priceless things,
each to be examined and admired for itself, for its peculiar qualities, that attitude is tempered by a realization
of the incompleteness of things by themselves. Miss
Bishop reveres spiritual toughness and courage, which are
won from life only by hard experience. Her poetic design
incorporates happily the particular and ordinary with the
fantastic and dreamlike, the brute actuality of behavior
with a penetrating moral perception. As she implies in
the last part of "The Monument," it is all done "to
cherish something"; that something, we know, is our
human life.

V

Brother Antoninus

(*William Everson*)

Catholic poetry, in the period of time this group of
studies attempts roughly to cover, originally saw its most
unique and accomplished practitioner in the person of
Robert Lowell. His first books, *Land of Unlikeness* and,
particularly, *Lord Weary's Castle*, revitalized orthodox
religious verse in this country, where one finds fewer
poets committed to such matters in their work than one
does in England. With its national church England continues to produce, even in an age of diminishing faith
and widespread agnosticism, poets who write, and write
well, from a firm core of Christian belief and thought.
America, on its side, has no persevering tradition of orthodox Christian poetry, though a heterodox religious
strain and a fierce moral sense are characteristic of American literature. In the twentieth century various experiments have been tried with religious poetry that involve
formal artistic innovation as well. T. S. Eliot epitomizes
this kind of experimentalist, but he has had no successful imitators; and Lowell, as the separate discussion of
him will show, travels away from the apocalyptic religious vision of his early poems to look more closely at
human life considered in itself, within a completely his-

orical and natural context. Of the Catholic poets who arrived in the same generation as Lowell, or a later one, only a limited number have made their Catholicism a central issue in their art or have evolved a specifically religious vision of experience as the distinctive source of poetic inspiration. Some of the best of them—John Frederick Nims, Ned O'Gorman, John Logan, Ernest Sanleen, Samuel Hazo—are identifiable as Catholics on those occasions when they do bring their poems to bear on the joys and vicissitudes of faith. The poems of Thomas Merton, a Trappist monk, tend to be projected outward and now chiefly to embrace, sometimes very forcefully and movingly, public and social dilemmas with their moral implications. By way of difference, the poetry of Brother Antoninus builds its foundations in the problems and conditions of his own life as an individual, both before and after his conversion to the Catholic church.

Only a portion of Brother Antoninus' career as a writer has been devoted to religious, specifically Catholic, poetry. His earlier reputation was created under his actual name of William Everson, and in examining this first part of his work we shall call him by that name, which appears on his books of those years. He made his debut with a small pamphlet of poems, *These Are the Ravens* (1935), and this secular half of his poetic career culminated in the representative volume of selected poems, *The Residual Years* (1948), published in his thirty-sixth year. Everson was born in Sacramento, California; his poetic vocation is undeniably associated with the Western states, where he has continued to live, to hold a variety of jobs, and to write. There also, for the past fifteen years, he has pursued his monastic vocation. After sporadic studying and a period of employment as a young man with the C.C.C. he returned to Fresno State College in the autumn of 1934 and was introduced to Robinson Jeffers' poetry, an encounter that signalled the beginning of his own poetic efforts. In a passage from a letter quoted by the publisher in his preface to *These Are the Ravens*, Everson says of his work:

> I like to feel that these poems are, with two or three exceptions, inherently of Fresno County. Although it was never my purpose to write of Fresno County, and although most of these poems could have been written in any section of the country, nevertheless the luxuriant vineyards, the heavy orchards, the miles of desolate pasture-lands, and back of it all the tremendous mountains heaved against the east, hold for me an appeal that I hope has crept into my verse.

Without any doubt this "appeal" is obvious in these early poems, and all to their advantage. In fact we should note here that many of the finest poems from both the secular and the religious parts of Everson's writing owe a great deal to their author's fondness for place and to his constant apprehension of what is involved in creation outside of man—in other words, the existence of birds, animals, trees; of soil and rock; of the behavior of the elements. His startling sensitivity to the created world may suddenly intrude upon the imagery of poems not otherwise concerned with such things, and yet what intrudes will seem at once to authenticate and support the less tangible regions of experience the poet is investigating. Probably this lesson was learned from Jeffers, though there exist similarities in this technique to two other poets with whom Everson has some affinity, Walt Whitman and D. H. Lawrence, who frequently interrupt the abstract and speculative with the concrete and descriptive. The beginning pieces, already metrically loose, display a feeling for location, a responsiveness to nature, through the poet's occupation as a worker on the land. "Winter Plowing" is a lyrical evocation of his tasks and surroundings:

Before my feet the plowshare rolls the earth,
Up and over,
Splitting the loam with a soft, tearing sound.
Between the horses I can see the red blur of a far
　　peach orchard,
Half obscured in drifting sheets of morning fog.
A score of blackbirds circles around me on shining
　　wings.
They alight beside me and scramble almost under
　　my feet
In search of upturned grubs.
The fragrance of the earth rises like a tule-pond
　　mist,
Shrouding me in impalpable folds of sweet, cool
　　smell,
Lulling my senses to the rhythm of the running
　　plow,
The jingle of the harness,
And the thin cries of the gleaming, bent-winged
　　birds.

Critics of Everson often speak of the presence of a
species of pantheism in his early work. While the regard
for earth, for the natural rhythms of life, or for the
biological cycle of birth, maturation, and death are especially plain, there appears to be very little mysticism
in the treatment of these themes. That is to say, the poet
does not venerate the physical universe and its processes,
or human physical life and its processes, as if they were
something divine, but rather brings them into the midst
of his poetic vocabulary because they comprise the essential reality with which he is involved and, at this
point, indicate the extent of the reality he knows and
believes in. Poetry, for Everson, should delineate his experience of this natural existence in all of its required
instinctive will and strength. The poet has at his disposal for the artistic labor the spiritual energies of con-

sciousness, imagination, and conscience; thus a poem
turns into the occasion for an exchange between the
spiritual and the natural in himself. This exchange is
maintained but intensified in the later religious poems,
where the spiritual takes on the added force of the supernatural, of Divine grace and command.

The dramatic tension arising from the interplay of
these powers, first in the poet and then in the poem,
doubtless accounts for the forcefully articulated quality
of speech we meet everywhere in his writings. This poetic
speech bears considerable weight, a weight derived from
the utmost sincerity and a passionate desire for exactitude; Everson attempts to grasp the ultimate truth his
language may be capable of yielding. But, we should understand, his motives on that side are not primarily aesthetic; and so his poetic manner is rough, sometimes
even awkward or in poor taste. Words twist, surge, and
lash out in his poems or, in other cases, they are formed
into massive, hewn blocks. At times Everson introduces
unfamiliar words or coins them, not out of pedantry, nor
with the idea of linguistic play we see in Wallace Stevens; instead he resembles an existentialist philosopher,
a Heidegger or Sartre, who tries to wrest new and difficult meanings from his experience. In a poem entitled
"The Roots" from his third collection, *The Masculine
Dead* (1942), he contemplates the history of the English
tongue from its origins. His attention fixes on the life
that has given shape and weight to the language through
centuries, invested it with untold emotions and significance. As the poem unfolds, his own relationship as a
writer to that language becomes apparent, and he finishes by defining his understanding of what a poem's
effect ought to be in the music of its words:

And I, not English, in a level valley of the last
    great west,
Watch from a room in the solstice weather,

And feel back of me trial and error,
The blunt sounds forming,
The importunate utterance of millions of men
Surge up for my ears,
The shape and color of all their awareness
Sung for my mind in the gust of their words.

A poem is alive, we take it with wonder,
Hardly aware of the roots of compulsion
Quickening the timbre of native sounds;
The ancient passion called up to being,
Slow and intense, haunting the rhythms of those
    spoken words.

In the body of his own art Everson has given us what
he calls in this same poem "the core of existence caught
on the tongue," though we should add that it is his own
existence he puts into his work, the persistent, uninhib-
ited investigation of himself as a man. To be sure, such
poems—and we come across them in his religious as well
as his secular writings—are precursors, with many of
Kenneth Rexroth's, of the autobiographical tendencies
prominent recently in the poetry of Robert Lowell or
Anne Sexton or Gary Snyder; but there is an objectification of most of the admittedly personal elements in
Everson's verse that sets it part from the confessional
bias of some later poets, and especially from the nearly
hysterical ravings of a number of San Francisco Beat
poets with whom he was later—under the name of
Brother Antoninus—linked. Then we must also acknowledge the fact that Everson did not occupy a position
from which to influence other writers; he has always be-
longed to the company of writers who had nothing to do
with Metaphysical wit, Laforguean irony, or with Symbolism and the use of mythology. His is a poetry of open
statement, tortured and driven by the poet's exhaustive
probing of himself.

In the later poems from *The Residual Years*, Everson includes a long sequence, "Chronicle of Division," which is his most intimate piece of writing if we are thinking of personal or private detail. This sequence covers his marriage, the separation imposed on the couple by the poet's imprisonment as a conscientious objector during World War II, an attempted reunion following his release, and then a final separation. Painful, haunting, and absolutely authentic, these poems resemble a diary in which are recorded the torments and self-searchings, the brief moments of pleasure, the slow destruction of a relationship: in other words, they provide a lengthy account of the inner man attempting to create a balance with his external circumstances. Yet the poems are not apologies for their author but serve instead as the means by which Everson can take hold of his experience in all honesty and give it form. He does not depart from this aesthetic strategy in his religious poetry. In place of such subjects as his marriage and separation we discover in *The Crooked Lines of God* (1959) that he has taken his personal spiritual condition as material for poetry or that he seeks an equivalent for this condition in Biblical and religious story. The same may be said in general for his latest volume, *The Hazards of Holiness* (1962), where, in a "Foreword," he clarifies some of his views on the act of writing. "A poem," he says, "like a dream, is 'whole' to the extent that it registers the mystery of the psychic complex which produced it. My poem can never be 'perfect' because I cannot be. If I ever achieve a 'victory over language' it can only be partial, and only to the extent that I have achieved a 'victory over myself.'" Whatever we may think of this notion—which seems to me to identify mistakenly the formal aesthetic perfection of a poem with the difficult, improbable spiritual perfection of the poet's life—it states boldly the moral and therapeutic character of the creative process as Everson sees it. And so we are not surprised when aesthetic criteria are also rejected a little further on. "Thus," he continues, "I can say truthfully that I have no interest in the conquest of language, as understood by those who seek to achieve a hypostatized aesthetic object. The victories I seek, those of 'appeasement and absolution, and something very near to annihilation,' are one and all victories over myself, the unremitting attempt to exorcize the demon."

These convictions about the motives and processes of poetic creation have only recently been formulated; therefore they need adjustment in our minds when we consider the earlier, and secular, poems of William Everson with their emphasis on the biological nature of human existence, the compulsive sexuality, the loneliness and frustration of individual endeavor unrelieved by any religious hope. Those themes echo throughout *The Residual Years*, and in the title poem of *The Masculine Dead*, not later reprinted, they are strongly combined. The speakers in the passage I shall quote are "the masculine dead," men who, prematurely deprived of life, lie underground like the dead of some Hardy or Housman poem dreaming on their past and on earthly existence as a whole. The device is highly artificial and purely poetical, for we are not meant to assume that these souls of the dead really survive in a spiritual realm by the will of a God. Everson has not yet settled on his Christian outlook and the position he takes here is fundamentally naturalistic. In the stanzas below he summarizes the entire cycle of mortal life as he envisages it during the first phase of his poetic career:

> And there rises before us the childhood moment
> When, staring out of wondering eyes,
> We saw the pattern open its folds,
> Show us the wide land lonely and broad between
>   the oceans,
> The little towns on the high plateaus,

Making so tiny a light in the dark,
We saw the forest of earth, and the long streets:
We saw the wind in the frozen tomb of the north,
And those tidal forces under the sea that alter the
      future;
And knew in the flare of that opening glimpse
The sudden awareness of what we were.

And it comes, it rises.
We see ourselves in the good strength,
Arrogant, loving our quick limbs and our wit,
Ignorant, singing our bawdy songs,
Shouting with pride and assurance in the plenty
      of our health.
Till over us crowded the load of darkness,
Slipping like shadow across the sun.
There was one long look of the turning sky,
And our knees caved, the spring-tight nerves
And the strained thews snapping and fraying,
And we fell, urine burned on our legs,
The broken lights and fragments of our dreams
Raced on our eyes;
Then only the night, shoreless,
The sea without sound,
Voiceless and soft.

We lay for a time on the edges of death
And watched the flesh slip into the earth.
We watched the eyes loosen their holds,
The brain that had hungered,
Known fury and pride,
Burned with lust and trembled with terror.
We saw our sex vanish, the passionate sperm,
All the future children of our loins
Be nothing, make mud,
A fertile place for the roots to plunder.
After a time the bones were chalk,

And the banded rings we wore on our fingers,
Corroded and green.

The distance from this vision of existence to the one
brought forward in the poems Everson began to write
after his conversion to Catholicism in 1949 is great in
some respects, and yet a decided continuity exists between the dilemmas posed by "Chronicle of Division,"
the ultimate pessimism of "The Masculine Dead," and
their resolution in a new way of life (fourteen months
with the Catholic Worker movement in 1950-51 and en-
trance into the Dominican Order following that) and
the poetry that grows out of it. Nonetheless, we should
not minimize the radical difference his changed beliefs
do make in his poetic themes and his human concerns;
if strains of somberness and of pain continue to show
themselves, they do so for altered reasons and against an
eternal rather than a temporal background.

The remarks quoted previously from *The Hazards
of Holiness* indicate that Brother Antoninus (as we shall
hereafter call him in correspondence with his newer
books and his monastic vocation) does not aim at formal innovation or aesthetic polish. In fact his poems frequently introduce materials that would seem to have
outlived their poetic—which is not to say theological or
moral—value except in the hands of an ambitious inno-
vator and formalist. The materials I refer to are Biblical
story and incident, and the lives of the saints. Yet
Brother Antoninus has given them new poetic spirit and
force without sliding into the traps of banality and cheap
piety. The reason for his success is that behind the re-
telling of familiar stories of the Wise Men and the shepherds, the birth of Jesus, the Flight in the Desert, the
agony of Gethsemane, and the Massacre of the Holy In-
nocents there stands the poet's own inner or spiritual circumstance which has, as he says, its peculiar relation to
each of these stories and the poems he has fashioned

from them. This relation can only become clear to us through a quality in the poems themselves, for there we meet the same intense voice which marks the earlier work speaking with an urgency, vividness, and singularity that give the stories a sudden life. Though certain of the poems articulate the sufferings and conflicts of a religious vocation devoutly obeyed, we still sense a deep and pervasive joy not present in *The Residual Years*.

Brother Antoninus writes poems that derive openly from his experience of the natural world as well as those dependent upon sacred history. In his love for the California coast and landscape there is no change except in perspective; he admires and marvels at the unspoiled life of creation, just as he did under the spell of Robinson Jeffers. But in a later poem such as "A Canticle to the Waterbirds," his new religious or supernatural perspective is surely alien to Jeffers'. This poem was "written for the Feast of Saint Francis of Assisi, 1950," and it is filled with the vitality and ecstasy we associate with Catholic visionary poets as different in other ways as Gerard Manley Hopkins, Paul Claudel, Edith Sitwell, and Ned O'Gorman, each of whom celebrates the particulars of God's creation:

> Clack your beaks you cormorants and kittiwakes,
> North on those rock-croppings finger-jutted into
>   the rough Pacific surge;
> You migratory terns and pipers who leave but the
>   temporal clawtrack written on sandbars there
>   of your presence;
> Grebes and pelicans; you comber-picking scoters
>   and you shorelong gulls;
> All you keepers of the coastline north of here to
>   the Mendocino beaches;
> All you beyond upon the cliff-face thwarting the
>   surf at Hecate Head;

Hovering the under-surge where the cold Colum-
     bia grapples at the bar;
North yet to the Sound, whose islands float like
     a sown flurry of chips upon the sea:
Break wide your harsh and salt-encrusted beaks
     unmade for song
And say a praise up to the Lord.

An awareness of nature as the actuality surrounding
crucial events and actions in sacred history appears in
those poems which treat aspects of the Christian story
and also, according to the poet's prefatory notes in *The
Crooked Lines of God*, obliquely reflect in their arrangement the developing stages of his own faith and monastic vocation. Natural detail is used in such a way as to
create the impression of contemporaneousness in what
is being described. In "The Flight in the Desert," for
instance, the setting with which the poem starts is,
strangely enough, some part of the American West; yet
Brother Antoninus allows the figures of Mary, Joseph,
and the infant Jesus to journey through this landscape
without a hint of incongruity or falsity. The poem, in
fact, gains substance and an atmosphere of reality from
this unusual transposition:

The last settlement scraggled out with a barbed
     wire fence
And fell from sight. They crossed the coyote
     country:
Mesquite, sage, the bunchgrass knotted in patches;
And there the prairie dog yapped in the valley;
And on the high plateau the short-armed badger
Delved his clay. But beyond that desert,
Raw, unslakable, its perjured dominion wholly
     contained
In the sun's remorseless mandate, where the dim
     trail

Died ahead in the watery horizon: God knows
    where.

That is the first stanza. The poem progresses slowly,
the long lines drawing each other on, reaches a section
which portrays the fleeing family, and then proceeds to
consider the effects suggested by the narrative. Once
again the religious perspective reveals itself. Here the
supernatural or Divine dimension of the story of the
Flight, which contains its full meaning and importance,
opens out beyond the human reality of the three trav-
elers on their difficult journey and returns to it, for that,
the poet seems to be telling us, is the manner of our
understanding. The landscape of these later stanzas is
still curiously modern and American, and the events that
take place, like those involved in them, appear both to
be historical and somehow to defeat history by coming
to life over and over again and in different locations—
or, it may be, everywhere and always. Brother Antoninus'
other poems based on sacred story leave the same odd
sensation.

> But they, the man and the anxious woman,
> Who stared pinch-eyed into the setting sun,
> They went forward into its denseness
> All apprehensive, and would many a time have
>   turned
> But for what they carried. That brought them on.
> In the gritty blanket they bore the world's great
>   risk,
> And knew it; and kept it covered, near to the
>   blind heart,
> That hugs in a bad hour its sweetest need,
> Possessed against the drawn night
> That comes now, over the dead arroyos.
> Cold and acrid and black.

This was the first of his goings forth into the
    wilderness of the world
There was much to follow: much of portent,
    much of dread.
But what was so meek then and so mere, so slight
    and strengthless,
(Too tender, almost, to be touched)—what they
    nervously guarded
Guarded them. As we, each day, from the lifted
    chalice
That strengthless Bread the mildest tongue sub-
    sumes,
To be taken out in the blatant kingdom,
Where Herod sweats, and his deft henchmen
Riffle the tabloids—that keeps us.

Over the campfire the desert moon
Slivers the west, too chaste and cleanly
To mean hard luck. The man rattles the skillet
To take the raw edge off the silence;
The woman lifts up her heart; the Infant
Knuckles the generous breast, and feeds.

Several poems in *The Crooked Lines of God* look to
the poet's private or inner experience rather than to the
life of Christ and the commemoration of saints as a fertile
area for imaginative concentration. "The Screed of the
Flesh," "The Encounter," "A Penitential Psalm," "Hos-
pice of the Word," "A Canticle to the Christ in the Holy
Eucharist," "Annul Me in My Manhood," and "Out of
the Ash" focus on a variety of spiritual problems in the
poet himself. Some of these poems, as well as a few addressed to saints, are heavily indebted to what Brother
Antoninus terms in his foreword "the erotic religious psychology of the Spanish Baroque," an overripe combination of sensuality and mysticism in which the approach

to God and the symbols of that approach are boldly
ambiguous. The better poems are, I believe, those favor-
ing austere renunciation and self-denial in a style that is
accordingly sparse and wiry. The erotic and baroque
poems appear heavy-handed and dull by contrast, bearing a foreign element that remains alien and unassimi-
lated. The harsh, lacerating speech of such a poem as
"Annul Me in My Manhood," or of "Sleep-Tossed I
Lie" (from *The Hazards of Holiness*) proves the inap-
propriateness of the baroque pieces:

>Sleep-tossed I lie,
>Midnight stemmed under,
>And the bloat moon
>Shut in its sky.
>
>Lord, Lord of these tangled sheets!
>My wrestling's witnesses
>Certify my heat.
>
>I have lain long, lain long,
>Long in thy grasp am lain,
>Lord of the midnight watchings,
>The monk's tongue-shuttered groan
>And the hermit's heart-ripped cry.
>
>Somewhere the wanton lovers keep
>Vigils of fecklessness,
>Their hearts
>Bursted on passion
>And the body's blade
>Plunged deep.
>And in that death find sleep.
>
>But I? Long have I lain,
>Long lain, and in the longing
>Fry.

Sleep-smooth this brow.
Bless with thy rippling breath
These anguish-awkward limbs.

Grant thy surcease.
Toy me no more, Lord.
Lord of the midnight wrestlings
Keep the peace!

This poem in its unabashed severity discloses the self-
scrutiny and the inward battles that generate some of the
best poems in Brother Antoninus' latest book. There is
also a very obvious infusion of violence in the new poetry,
a violence the poet has defended in a "Dialogue on Holy
Violence" with Albert Fowler in the magazine *Approach*
(Fall 1963), remarking that his religious experience has
involved him in it, and that he has consequently trans-
ferred it to his poems. This defense seems to me perfectly
legitimate in most cases, though a few poems, and "The
Hazards of Holiness" in particular, are pointlessly sadistic
in detail. However, the largest part of Brother Antoninus'
recent work attempts to objectify in word and image the
poet's inner world where the struggle for his faith is carried out. Internal division, the endless demands imposed
by the flesh, the desire for union with God and the
equally powerful instinct to escape Him, self-assertion
versus self-effacement: these are the themes that inspire
the most durable poems here. Biblical subjects do appear
a few times (in "Jacob and the Angel," "The Conversion
of St. Paul," and "The Hazards of Holiness"), but this
vein was generally exhausted by the previous book and
now has a slight air of irrelevance. The chief accomplishment in the most recent volume is not to be found in the
longer poems, nor in a continued reliance on sacred story,
but in those brief, taut poems—"I Am Long Weaned" is
a good example—torn by suffering, self-doubt, and the
pangs induced by true religious belief:

I am long weaned.

My mouth, puckered on gall,
Sucks dry curd.

My thoughts, those sterile watercourses
Scarring a desert.

My throat is lean meat.
In my belly no substance is,
Nor water moves.

My gut goes down
A straight drop to my groin.

My cod is withered string,
My seed, two flints in a sack.

Some day, in some other place,
Will come a rain;
Will come water out of deep wells,
Will come melons sweet from the vine.

I will know God.

Sophia, deep wisdom,
The splendid unquenchable fount:

Unbind those breasts.

These bare, tormented lines give full voice to Brother
Antoninus' existence and to the faith he embraces; with
the honesty characteristic of his poetry from its inception,
he faces the realities in which he finds himself situated
and those others, supernatural ones, which he hopes for
and trusts in. His road as a Catholic poet has not been
very easy, but his achievement must make us grateful
that he chose it.

VI

Karl Shapiro

Karl Shapiro, and most other American poets who began to publish and make themselves known in the late 1930's and early 1940's, could not help but be influenced by the example and practice of such English writers, just barely their seniors, as W. H. Auden, Stephen Spender, C. Day Lewis, and Louis MacNeice. Not only did Auden, in particular, wield influence in idiom and style, but also in his merciless psychological analysis and moral criticism of capitalistic society, reflected in his writings during the Depression, the Spanish Civil War, and the rise of Nazi Germany. Though a wide current of private meanings and covert references flows through his early verse—also picked up by some younger poets but seldom handled with anything approaching Auden's skill and dexterity—the elements of social revolution, satire, and moral judgment remain prominent.

Auden's ideas may seem to be confused in his first books between psychoanalysis, Marxist theory of history, and a personal belief in love and individual integrity as the means of defeating human sickness; yet the reader can never doubt for a minute that this poet is committed to the realities of his situation in time and place. Though

Eliot and Pound had few direct imitators among the poets of this generation, Auden and his friends had them in plenty. Again, it is the open involvement of these English poets with the actual world of institutions, ideologies, technology, and urbanization that seemed bold and attractive to other writers. American poets of this period— Muriel Rukeyser, Delmore Schwartz, John Berryman, Weldon Kees, Shapiro himself, to name a few—who began to struggle one way or another in their art with the life of contemporary society, were surely indebted to the English poets named, but such influences merely served, in their case, for an apprenticeship from which they graduated to independent and variegated poetic speech.

A second influence worth noting depends upon individual participation in the war. World War II was sensed in advance by many writers such as Yeats, Auden, Kunitz, Berryman, and others, who expressed the growing mood of tension and foreboding in their verse, frequently supplementing it with visions of cosmic disaster. These premonitions of war, rumors of collapse in Western society, and murmurs and threats of social revolution became integral to most poets' perceptions of reality. Poetry, by the fusion of imagination and conscience into a poem's moral imperative, actually became a mode of acting in the world. This literary atmosphere is the one in which Karl Shapiro's poetic talent came to birth and was nourished. Out of this literary and social situation his first collection appeared in 1942, published while its author was on active military duty in the Pacific. (I leave out of account an earlier book, privately printed.) After *Person, Place and Thing* he was to write and publish two more books, *V-Letter* (1944) and *Essay on Rime* (1945), before his return to the United States and his discharge. He fell heir to the two influences discussed above, and yet he was not mastered by them. Shapiro has always shown the power of imagination and will to

seek his own desired goals as a poet; the latest phase of
his work, beginning with *Poems of a Jew* (1958) and continuing to his recent *The Bourgeois Poet* (1964), proves
his ability to travel alone and to reject his literary past.

But Shapiro's initial book gives us little cause to think
that he would veer so radically in this later direction. In
these poems he operates very smoothly and compellingly
within an idiom that was in some part the creation of
Auden; and he makes this idiom his own, lends it a personal finish. As the title *Person, Place and Thing* implies,
Shapiro takes a poetic stance in the midst of the very
definite everyday world. His manner is straightforward—
with no unusual difficulties of symbolism or learned reference, no oddities of style. The poems are clearly statements of an alert, intelligent, and humane person who
unabashedly concentrates on things as they are; that is,
they reflect the knowledge and experience of a man
thoroughly aware of his time and his surroundings.
Through his perceivings and discriminations in each
poem, a precise picture of the world takes shape. We
cannot fail to notice either, with the very first poem in
the book, that the cast of Shapiro's mind can be critical
and ironic; the opening lines of "Scyros" are sufficiently
convincing:

> The doctor punched my vein
> The captain called me Cain
> Upon my belly sat the sow of fear
> With coins on either eye
> The President came by
> And whispered to the braid what none could hear

Self-revelation and self-characterization of the poet
when they appear in Shapiro's poems are not, as they are
in Robert Lowell's *Life Studies*, the center of interest,
though perhaps we need to except a few pieces from
The Bourgeois Poet; rather, the poet occupies a position
of dramatic convenience, a route of access to the primary

material of the poem, whatever that happens to be. If there is biographical disclosure in Shapiro's work, it aims to be representative rather than merely subjective. Movement is very often outward from the speaker to external reality; or a poem may have that reality impose itself upon the speaker, who is a representative individual or conscience. This should not, however, suggest that the speaker's voice lacks particular identity, but that it does not usually take such identity as a subject or a theme. We discover Shapiro assuming, not his own part, but the *human* one in his poems; in this he recalls the later Kunitz, whose voice is often prompted to speech on *man's* behalf. Thus, to pick a single instance, the title poem of *V-Letter*, while it surely contains details from its author's own life and relationships, becomes more than a love poem from one certain individual to another; we see it at last as the statement of almost any soldier in such circumstances. Yet Shapiro never sacrifices the concreteness that properly belongs to the poem, nor does he employ gimmicks to give it a spurious universality.

The concern with external reality or the public world in Shapiro's writing fastens with some frequency on different aspects of American life. The titles of his poems quickly illustrate this preoccupation: "Buick," "The Dome of Sunday," "Property," "Washington Cathedral," "Alexandria," "Hollywood," "Drug Store." Poets such as Eliot and Pound included particulars of environment in some of their poems, but these were used to enhance a general atmosphere. In Shapiro, as in Auden and MacNeice, these particulars are often brought into the foreground of the poem, where they are looked at for themselves or as inseparable, if not always desirable, ingredients of modern experience. The attitude required of a poet undertaking such observation and assessment is, I suppose, basically a moral one, though not moral in any trite or platitudinous sense. Other requirements, which Shapiro easily fulfills, are a gift for the satirical and a lightness of

manner. His temperament is relaxed as a rule, even in
many of his polemics, with genuine sympathy for what
is natural and human in experience. He distrusts "The
Intellectual," as he says so bluntly in the poem of that
title: "I'd rather be a barber and cut hair/Than walk
with you in gilt museum halls. . . ." So we should have
no trouble understanding this poet's distaste for pretense, his resigned but ironical appraisal of the privi-
leged and the poor as he envisages them buried together
in "Necropolis":

> Even in death they prosper; even in the death
> Where lust lies senseless and pride fallow
> The mouldering owners of rents and labor
> Prosper and improve the high hill.
>
> For theirs is the stone whose name is deepest cut;
> Theirs the facsimile temple, theirs
> The iron acanthus and the hackneyed Latin,
> The boxwood rows and all the birds.
>
> And even in death the poor are thickly herded
> In intimate congestion under streets and alleys.
> Look at the standard sculpture, the cheap
> Synonymous slabs, the machined crosses.
>
> Yes, even in death the cities are unplanned.
> The heirs govern from the old centers;
> They will not remove. And the ludicrous angels,
> Remains of the poor, will never fly
> But only multiply in the green grass.

Many of the poets of the generation preceding Shapiro's (and Auden's), poets of the post-Symbolist period,
thoroughly lamented the growth of urban and technological society with its spiritual deficit and looked back
longingly to an idealized past, the classical world of
Greece or the mediæval Christian world of Dante. Al-

though some of Shapiro's contemporaries, such as Roethke and Eberhart, show religious and mystical inclinations in parts of their work, none has expressed a historical nostalgia in the manner of Yeats, Pound, and Eliot. Shapiro is obviously historically aware, and not merely in his poems about military life—which are not so numerous in his work as in Jarrell's—but in most poems whose subjects have an historical dimension that he can meaningfully explore. Yet this historical dimension does not lead to contrasts between the past and the present that ignore the imperfections of the former and discredit the latter altogether. I believe Shapiro would say that such an effort is, in any case, not a poet's business, though it might be a historian's or a philosopher's. A poet's business is not with culture either, he has insisted in his prose works, *Beyond Criticism* (1953) and in *In Defense of Ignorance* (1960); the poet's true affair is only with poetry. Shapiro introduces history into a poem as it helps to explain the present, whether his aim is praise or criticism; and he supplies those historical details which bear specifically on his subject. His poem "University" exemplifies this approach and also demonstrates the author's capacity for tough moral criticism and barbed satirical jabs:

> To hurt the Negro and avoid the Jew
> Is the curriculum. In mid-September
> The entering boys, identified by hats,
> Wander in a maze of mannered brick
>   Where boxwood and magnolia brood
>   And columns with imperious stance
>   Like rows of ante-bellum girls
>   Eye them, outlanders.
>
> In whited cells, on lawns equipped for peace,
> Under the arch, and lofty banister,
> Equals shake hands, unequals blankly pass;
> The exemplary weather whispers, "Quiet, quiet"

And visitors on tiptoe leave
For the raw North, the unfinished West,
As the young, detecting an advantage,
     Practice a face.

Where, on their separate hill, the colleges,
Like manor houses of an older law,
Gaze down embankments on a land in fee,
The Deans, dry spinsters over family plate,
     Ring out the English name like coin,
     Humor the snob and lure the lout.
     Within the precincts of this world
         Poise is a club.

But on the neighboring range, misty and high,
The past is absolute: some luckless race
Dull with inbreeding and conformity
Wears out its heart and comes barefoot and bad
     For charity or jail. The scholar
     Sanctions their obsolete disease;
     The gentleman revolts with shame
         At his ancestor.

And the true nobleman, once a democrat,
Sleeps on his private mountain. He was one
Whose thought was shapely and whose dream was
     broad;
This school he held his art and epitaph.
     But now it takes from him his name,
     Falls open like a dishonest look,
     And shows us, rotted and endowed,
         Its senile pleasure.

Here the present and past are juxtaposed, but not, as
it might look at a glance, for the purpose of contrasting
the splendor of former times with the ethical weakness
and social corruption of the modern age. Though Jeffer-

son's "dream" is shown to have come to a different end
than he planned, it is still only with reference to his life,
thought, and character that the poet can discover any
ideals in the past. Otherwise, the implication seems to be,
historical conditions, customs, prejudices, have formed
this university as it is today, with its instinctive contempt
for racial minorities, its neglect of the poor whites (the
"luckless race" of hill people), its morally neutral scholar-
ship, its continuation of pre-Civil War attitudes and the
active transmission of them to its members and students,
its encouragement of hypocrisy and falsity in those it
teaches by means of sanctioned but reprehensible tradi-
tions ("the young, detecting an advantage,/Practice a
face").

Shapiro likes to use poetically what presents itself in
the course of daily experience, and thus to achieve that
representativeness of which we have spoken. He scruti-
nizes intensely, though not without humor and sympathy,
the places he visits, whether Melbourne, Australia, or
Washington, D. C. American customs and institutions
fall beneath this steady gaze, and so do a great variety
of type-figures, whom he examines with care in as many
ways as he has subjects. Some of these figures permit
him to indulge a talent for the grotesque and the irrational, qualities that come into prominence later in *The
Bourgeois Poet* but which appear earlier in "The Glutton," "The Fly," "The Gun," and other poems. The
beginning stanzas of "The Glutton," from *Person, Place
and Thing* prove his early desire to try this talent for the
monstrous caricature:

> The jowls of his belly crawl and swell like the sea
> When his mandibles oily with lust champ and go
>   wide;
> Eternal, the springs of his spittle leak at the lips
> Suspending the tongue like a whale that rolls on
>   the tide.

His hands are as rotten fruit. His teeth are as corn.
Deep are the wells of his eyes and like navels, blind
Dough is the brain that supplies his passion with
    bread
Dough is the loose-slung sack of his great behind.

In Shapiro's recent prose poems the technique of the
grotesque becomes a practical one for conveying something of the enormity of contemporary urban existence
and the business corporation milieu without confinement
to a single figure as the center of focus. The following
poem, number 8 from *The Bourgeois Poet*, attempts to
depict the character of this life, its vulgarity and horror
and artificiality, through attention to pertinent and revealing details or objects, fragments of the general experience, and a semi-surrealistic mode of presentation. The
result may call to mind Chaplin's *Modern Times* and
Kafka's fiction in the mixture of feelings—satirical laughter and moral revulsion—it arouses, but it is still very
much Shapiro's vision; the reality it explores belongs to
this country at this moment in time. We can estimate
the distance Shapiro has covered, stylistically, from his
previous work by comparing this prose poem with "The
Glutton."

Office love, love of money and fight, love of calcu-
    lated sex. The offices reek with thin volcanic
    metal. Tears fall in typewriters like drops of sol-
    der. Brimstone of brassieres, low voices, the whirr
    of dead-serious play. From the tropical tree and
    the Rothko in the Board Room to the ungram-
    matical broom closet fragrant with waxes, to the
    vast typing-pool where coffee is being served by
    dainty waitresses maneuvering their handtrucks,
    music almost unnoticeable falls. The very tele-
    phones are hard and kissable, the electric water-
    cooler sweetly sweats. Gold simmers to a boil in
    braceleted arms and sunburned cheeks. What

ritual politeness nevertheless, what subtlety of clothing. And if glances meet, if shoulders graze, there's no harm done. Flowers, celebrations, pregnancy leave, how the little diamonds sparkle under the psychologically soft-colored ceilings. It's an elegant windowless world of soft pressures and efficiency joys, of civilized mishaps—mere runs in the stocking, papercuts.

Where the big boys sit the language is rougher. Phone calls to China and a private shower. No paper visible anywhere. Policy is decided by word of mouth like gangsters. There the power lies and is sexless.

Grotesque effects are created in this piece with less aesthetic self-consciousness, which is to say, with less obvious care for the artistic surface as something to be regarded for itself, and with more commitment to the actuality of the life disclosed, than they are in "The Glutton." The earlier poem attracts us in part because of its dazzling linguistic and musical performance; the later one forsakes the opportunity for such a display in order to try out subtler devices and rhythms and to allow concentration on the thing presented without much distraction. As satire, the prose poem thrusts deeper and is, in its surrealistic perceptions, the more realistic of the two.

Discussion of the satirical and grotesque elements in Shapiro's writing should not blind us to the personal attitude manifest in those other poems which formulate the values and temper the emotions underlying the criticisms he does make. That attitude is the one I indicated when I said that Shapiro always takes the *human* part or role in his poems—and does it in the teeth of the same world that he faces in his satires. "Auto Wreck," which is again

one of his early, but also one of his best, poems, illustrates the meaning of this human part. The poem starts
after the wreck has occurred, and its opening disarms us
with a wonderfully lyrical description of the ambulance
coming from afar toward the scene of the accident:

> Its quick soft silver bell beating, beating,
> And down the dark one ruby flare
> Pulsing out red light like an artery,
> The ambulance at top speed floating down
> Past beacons and illuminated clocks
> Wings in a heavy curve, dips down,
> And breaks speed, entering the crowd.

These lines are effective, to be sure, yet they remain on
what I shall call, for lack of a better phrase, a purely
lyrical plane, a level at which we can enjoy the imagery
for its sheer beauty because we have still to be acquainted
with the connected events. Shapiro has so far withheld
details of the disaster. And as the stanza continues with
its muted account of the efficiency of the ambulance and
its crew we are not brought much closer to the accident;
only two words stand out as startling indicators of the
occasion's horror: "mangled" and "terrible." In them we
can see something of the human depths stirred by what
has taken place. Shapiro has, of course, used these words
to awaken our expectations and to prepare us for what
really interests him but won't appear until the second
stanza—the accident's aftermath. With that stanza, point
of view in the poem is also clarified. While Shapiro is
plainly the speaker, he employs the collective "we," thus
implying that he speaks for the other bystanders as well
as for himself, and that he is articulating what they
merely feel and think. Such an implication adds considerable force and range to his own voice. Furthermore,
it gives a full human resonance to the awe, the terror,
and the questioning of poet and spectators alike:

We are deranged, walking among the cops
Who sweep glass and are large and composed.
One is still making notes under the light.
One with a bucket douches ponds of blood
Into the street and gutter.
One hangs lanterns on the wrecks that cling,
Empty husks of locusts, to iron poles.

Our throats were tight as tourniquets,
Our feet were bound with splints, but now,
Like convalescents intimate and gauche,
We speak through sickly smiles and warn
With the stubborn saw of common sense,
The grim joke and the banal resolution.
The traffic moves around with care,
But we remain, touching a wound
That opens to our richest horror.
Already old, the question Who shall die?
Becomes unspoken Who is innocent?
For death in war is done by hands;
Suicide has cause and still birth, logic;
And cancer, simple as a flower, blooms.
But this invites the occult mind,
Cancels our physics with a sneer,
And spatters all we know of denouement
Across the expedient and wicked stones.

The poem moves through these two stanzas to its climactic point—the question about violent and chance death, death that strikes suddenly and without any discernible reason. It is characteristic of Shapiro to proceed toward some larger theme beyond his immediate poetic subject. The unexpected auto crash, the pain and death, are not directly shown; emphasis is put, less sensationally, on the aftermath, from which we are easily able to reconstruct as much of the catastrophe itself as is necessary. Shapiro has no wish to render the victims' experience.

More subtly, he wants to investigate the *second* collision
—the impact of this apparently senseless accident on the
logical operations of the spectators' minds, and the emotions aroused by that impact. The knowledge urged on
those at the scene, the poet believes, defeats any reason-
ing and invites darker speculations, which even hint at
ideas of innocence, guilt, and retribution. Reason and
knowledge are destroyed in the very event ("And spatters
all we know of denouement/Across the expedient and
wicked stones"). The significance of the poem lies in the
discovery of the inexplicable that the auto wreck makes
possible. Shapiro's bafflement is the same as the other
witnesses', and so he proffers no conclusions to comfort
us. Since he refuses to turn to any metaphysical or religious explanations, he can only register a shrewd but
perfectly human admission of the inadequacy of our
minds before such tragic facts.

A similar condition of pain and loss, though not of
death, attracts Shapiro's efforts in another of his best
poems, "The Leg." Again the poet as speaker gives over
his voice to another individual's thoughts and feelings;
this time, however, he identifies himself with the situation
of the victim, a soldier who awakens in a hospital to find
that his leg has been amputated. But if Shapiro is imagi-
natively capable of entering the life of this young soldier,
he also wants to keep his own voice distinguishable and
a part of his separate identity, so that it can emerge to
speak for him in the closing meditative stanza. Therefore
Shapiro uses the third person as a narrative device and yet
can make himself seem to be a kind of presence absorbed
in the soldier's inner experience, a sympathetic and vocal
consciousness which momentarily inhabits the soldier's
world of suffering and adjustment.

At the start of the poem the wounded soldier floats
slowly upward to awareness, but still in "twilight sleep"
he knows that he has lost something. Between the first
and second stanzas there is an indefinite passage of time

which permits the patient, in the latter one, to arrive at the stage of recognizing his deprivation: ". . . he will know it's gone,/O where! and begin to tremble and cry." In the next stanza he has begun to live with his injury, to come to terms with his own altered shape in a curiously—but how necessarily!—amiable way:

> He learns a shape
> That is comfortable and tucked in like a sock.
> This has a sense of humor, this can despise
> The finest surgical limb, the dignity of limping,
> The nonsense of wheel-chairs. Now he smiles to the wall.
> The amputation becomes an acquisition.

There follows a reversal of the established manner of thinking about this injury. Shapiro changes briefly to the point of view of the severed leg itself and sees it as "wondering where he [the soldier] is. . . ." The man who has endured this loss is not the only victim in the light of the reversal; the soldier is transformed into the leg's "injury," and "the leg is the orphan." A notion of the profound organic unity of the self, of the physical and the spiritual, arises in the last half of this stanza and becomes a vision of the fundamental nature of reality, religious in character and requiring our devotion. Babette Deutsch, in her *Poetry in Our Time*, has remarked with reference to another of Shapiro's poems that it exhibits a strain of thought probably influenced by Rilke; this view holds, in the German poet's words (as translated by Miss Deutsch), that "all life is lived" by all creatures and things, which means, as Shapiro is saying in "The Leg," that the lost leg has its own life, is not simply a dead, cast-off appendage, though it exists properly in relation to the whole self, the body and spirit of the soldier. As the poem progresses toward its finish, Shapiro first recommends that the crippled soldier "pray for its [the leg's] safety,/And after a little it will die quietly"; then in the closing stanza he offers his own prayer, which submits an interpretation of the body as a reminder of the spiritual, a token of God's creative power as the origin of our being:

> The body, what is it, Father, but a sign
> To love the force that grows in us, to give back
> What in Thy palm is senselessness and mud?
> Knead, knead the substance of our understanding
> Which must be beautiful in flesh to walk
> That if Thou take me angrily in hand
> And hurl me to the shark, I shall not die!

Unlike "Auto Wreck," this poem finds a resolution in the transcendent Divine "force that grows in us" and explains the purpose of suffering as a means of recalling our attention to that force. The ending lines of religious supplication, very moving in themselves, express an attitude we seldom come across in any such overt form in Shapiro's writing. This poet is not too explicit, as he does not have to be, about his ultimate beliefs, but I think it is fair to say that he generally displays a strong aversion to religious doctrines and institutions (in spite of a few poems that testify to a momentary attraction to Catholicism). In the closest he has ventured to straight autobiographical poetry until The Bourgeois Poet, a group of lyrics called "Recapitulations," published in their entirety in Trial of a Poet (1947), he describes his wedding, and the beliefs of his bride and himself:

> The atheist bride is dressed in blue,
> The heretic groom in olive-drab,
> The rabbi, of more somber hue,
> Arrives upon the scene by cab.

Shapiro's later essays plainly state their distaste for the orthodoxy of Eliot and the homemade philosophy of Yeats' A Vision. It is probably best to think of him as a poet whose particular attitudes or positions depend upon the ordering of an individual experience that the composition of each poem demands. Thus he remains true to the feeling of terrified puzzlement resulting from the events of "Auto Wreck"; and in "The Leg" his thought leads him from contemplation of a single physical injury to a vision of the bond between material bodies and spiritual nature. Both poems are dictated by an emotional honesty and an understanding that belong to their separate occasions. Shapiro's quest for accurate and unhindered perception is the implicit justification for this poetic method. And so his is the way of sympathetic identification, though he manages to keep a certain valuable detachment through irony. Shapiro matured in a period when myth, due to the influence of Yeats, Eliot, and others, was all the rage, but he avoided the imitation of these predecessors. His one "mythological" work did not appear in a book until the publication of his selected *Poems 1940-1953*. This cycle of poems, entitled "Adam and Eve," he writes in a note in *Poems of a Jew* (1958), where it is reprinted, consists of pieces that "are not symbolic but literal interpretations. That is, I wrote them according to my own interpretation of the lines in Genesis, where they are first presented." We are supposed to read these poems just as we do his others, as direct interpretations of an experience—in this case, not an auto wreck or an amputation, but the experience of reading Genesis.

Ultimately, Shapiro refuses everything but fidelity to his own experience, his perceptions and ideas. His writing over the past few years is the best illustration. In his volume of polemical essays, *In Defense of Ignorance*, and his latest book of prose poems, *The Bourgeois Poet*, he vigorously severs most of his past allegiances and associations. He washes his hands of the dominant tradition in modernist poetry, particularly the work of Eliot and Pound. Though some of his judgments appear arbitrary, there is courage and frankness in his manner. And some of his opinions have a freshness and an incisive quality that are positively healthy. Shapiro's rebelliousness actually stems from a greater about-face than he bothers to admit. If he now praises D. H. Lawrence as a poet—and we can agree with much of the praise—he doesn't trouble to remind us of his scathing poem "D.H.L." from *V-Letter*, which censures the English writer for his lack of humanity. Likewise, the debt to Auden in his early poems goes further than his confession of it in *In Defense of Ignorance* suggests.

This change assumes tangible artistic form in *The Bourgeois Poet*. As Lowell does in some of the pieces in his *Life Studies*, Shapiro breaks with accepted metrical patterns to attempt a stark poetry of direct speech. But Shapiro goes beyond the experiments of Lowell, and those of Robert Bly, James Wright, John Ashbery, or Frank O'Hara; he tackles the difficult form of the prose poem, composed not in broken lines or irregular stanzas, but in prose paragraphs. If we look for a precedent in his earlier writing, we will come upon two prose poems, "The New Ring" and "The Dirty Word," in *Trial of a Poet*. We can estimate Shapiro's seriousness in turning completely in that direction by noticing how he has chosen "The Dirty Word" for inclusion as his favorite piece of work in Paul Engle's and Joseph Langland's anthology *Poet's Choice* (1963). Commenting on his selection, Shapiro says:

> Why must grown people listen to rhymes? Why must meters be tapped out on nursery drums? Why hasn't America won the battle of Iambic Five? When are we going to grow up?
>
> I wrote "The Dirty Word" almost twenty years ago and others in the same vein, yet it has taken me a lifetime to wear this form like my own coat. In those days I was just trying it on. Now I

feel ashamed when I write meter and rhyme, or dirty, as if I were wearing a dress.

The extremity of this statement may understandably prevent a number of readers from accepting it objectively, but there is no doubt in my mind that it springs from Shapiro's most fundamental emotions with respect to his art. We should, then, view it as a statement of personal intention, rather than a judgment having widespread validity. But for Shapiro it is an aesthetic declaration; after twenty years the prose poem has come to be for him a more genuine and natural artistic form. In a recent paper that asks, "Is Poetry an American Art?" (*College English*, March 1964), he decides it is not. For Americans, "trying to write poetry in the old manner is murder," and we are treated to his version of the struggles, apparently judged unsuccessful, of Cummings, Jeffers, Roethke, Marianne Moore, and others, to "produce a poetry of sensibility." The alternative is "the heaven of prose," which Shapiro says we do contribute to. Here are some of his summary remarks:

> I am in earnest when I argue that American poetry is yet to be born and that what we have optimistically called our poetry is only a garden of chemical flowers. I share the responsibility with Whitman, who laid it on the line when he denied the possibility of a formal poetics in America. I elicit the support of Eliot who shrewdly named Whitman a great prose writer. Pound who demonstrated how the Old World forms might be broken. Williams who struggled so long to locate in language the rhythm of American life at its worst.

In applying himself to the form of the prose poem, which has only occasionally been tried by American poets, Shapiro is mapping one possible road to follow. Not only is he drawing on the support of Eliot, Pound, Whitman, and Williams, but he is coming close to the solid French tradition of the prose poem and is perhaps learning something from poets like Baudelaire, Leon-Paul Fargue, Max Jacob, St.-John Perse, Henri Michaux, and René Char who have added so much to its development. Given the plastic nature of the prose poem (which doesn't make it any easier to write), it provides certain opportunities to handle experience differently, with less sacrifice to the demands of poetic formality and convention. Baudelaire, in the preface to his *Le Spleen de Paris*, points out some of the advantages to be gained in the prose poem. "Which one of us," he writes, addressing himself to the problem, "has not, on his ambitious days, dreamed of the miracle of a poetic prose, musical without rhyme or rhythm, supple enough and striking enough to adapt itself to the lyrical movements of the soul, to the undulations of revery, to the surge of consciousness?" It is just these sorts of advantages that Shapiro seeks, and has won for himself to a degree in *The Bourgeois Poet*: a literary technique that combines the freedom of prose with the brevity, the attention to word, image, and music associated with poetry.

The Bourgeois Poet definitely has about it the air of a new imaginative release. Irony and social criticism are still there, but autobiography, invective, heavy doses of sexuality, often dominated by an atmosphere of the dream and of irrationality, and an occasional prophetic note are now blended together. Unquestionably, an energy and a frankness that were formerly constrained have become primary agents of this altered poetry. Because of their length—and they are ruined by presentation in bits and fragments—the prose poems must be sparingly quoted here; besides, *The Bourgeois Poet* has to be read through as a book, even though it contains no strong narrative thread. It is not a uniformly good book, but the pieces that make it up belong together and give a cumulative impression. Then again it is a book we should not try to decide about at once; it will take some getting used to.

But I would like to include another of these prose poems by way of ending—though with Shapiro it is a beginning—and as an illustration of the effects he can create. In this poem Shapiro is once more identified with what happens, but he also remains the observer and commentator. The paragraphs of the prose poem allow for the juxtaposition of different but related elements, so there is not always an obvious line of narration or of logical continuity. The treatment of the material itself within the paragraphs likewise differs from ordinary straightforward prose in being more compressed and highly charged with feeling, more abrupt and elliptical. The aim is to present rather than to explain. The subtleties and nuances are those of a more conventional poetry but arranged within another framework. Beyond such remarks we will have to let Shapiro's prose poems speak for themselves. To close, here is poem 23 from *The Bourgeois Poet*, in which the narrator evocatively describes an experience but leaves it without comment to our own feeling for its peculiar suggestiveness:

> From the top floor of the Tulsa hotel I gaze at the night beauty of the cracking-plant. Candlelit city of small gas flames by the thousands, what a lovely anachronism dancing below like an adolescent's dream of the 1880's, the holy gas redeemed from Baudelaire's mustachioed curses. Elsewhere are the white lights of the age, but here, like a millionaire who frowns on electricity, the opulence of flame. Descending on Rome from the air at night, a similar beauty: the weak Italian bulbs like faulty rheostats yellowly outline the baroque curves of the Tiber, the semicircles of the monstrous Vatican, endless broken parabolas.

The cracking-plant is equally palatial. Those oil men in the silent elevator, like princes with their voices of natural volume, their soft hats and their name-drops (like the balloons of words in the mouths of caricatures in political cartoons), men of many mansions. The doors of the room are mahogany. Through one which adjoins and is locked I hear the guttural laughter of undress, neither leisurely nor quick, indistinct wording, and all is silent but a woman's moan. Now it rises like the grip of pain; it is almost loud; it is certainly sincere, like the pent-up grief of deep relief; now it is round, now vibrant, now it is scaly as it grows. (Then it steps off into nothingness.)

I stand awed in my stocking-feet and move respectfully toward the window, as a man in an art gallery moves toward a more distant masterpiece to avoid the musical chatter of intruders. The cracking-plant sails on through the delicate Oklahoma night, flying the thousand hot flags of Laputa.

VII

Isabella Gardner

"Writing poetry," Isabella Gardner says in the title of a recent poem that leads right into its opening lines, "is a game that no one quits while he or she's ahead. The/ stakes are steep." And though she, like Elizabeth Bishop, has been slow to publish, Miss Gardner is still, to keep to her metaphor, running ahead of the game. In the first of her two books, *Birthdays from the Ocean* (1955), she established her indisputable claim to natural gifts any poet would be proud to possess. The most obvious of these are her love for words—the ability to use them freely and unself-consciously, and with a gay vitality that recalls Dylan Thomas and E. E. Cummings—and her innate rhythmic sense. Of the women poets who are her approximate contemporaries only a few, such as Muriel Rukeyser, Jean Garrigue, and the late Sylvia Plath in her final poems, could rival her energy in handling words. In Miss Gardner's work the rhythmic movement and the richness of language merge to fashion a sturdy but flexible musical idiom completely her own; and the poet is not afraid to permit it the utmost liberty of sensuous play. Her short poem "Cadenza" even borrows its title from a light musical flourish:

Conjure away the blue and the dim and the dark
    cloths
I am no longer in the night or the half light
I want a shout of white and an aria of fire
and a paean of green and a coral carillon
not Cinderella's slippers not the Emperor's new
    clothes
not the skull behind the flower but the bone that
    is the rose.

The absence of punctuation here—it is occasionally
very sparse in Miss Gardner's poetry—is worth noticing
because it leaves the task of ordering the flow of the poem
at least partially up to the reader, who is, by this tactic,
fully engaged with its language and rhythm. Reading
these poems requires an active participation that truly re-
creates them in the mind. "Summers Ago," a later poem
dedicated to Edith Sitwell, herself an expert at musical
wordplay in verse, illustrates in just a few of its lines the
persistence of the author's musical talents:

Children I told you I tell you our sun was a hail of
    gold!
I say that sun stoned, that sun stormed our tran-
    quil, our blue bay
bellsweet saltfresh water (bluer than tongue-can-
    tell, daughter)
and dazed us, darlings, and dazzled us. . . .

The exuberant voice that resounds throughout Isabella
Gardner's poetry has its origins in these musical propensities, and they endow her work with a refreshing buoy-
ancy. But the inclinations carry their own dangers; too
great a facility can damage poems by letting them become
excuses for mere stylistic exercise, brilliant perhaps, and
fanciful, but weak in meaning. Such chances are courageously taken by Miss Gardner, and her lapses are sur-
prisingly rare, particularly when measured by the risks.

Even more important, she can think concretely *in* the words and images she disposes, a habit that allows her to try always to increase the capacity of her language, to enlarge the range of suggestiveness and connotation in a poem. Miss Gardner seems at certain times to wish that her words could break all bonds and confinements, soar beyond restriction, but she knows too the impossibility of such freedom, which can quickly transform itself into a kind of captivity. In his collection of essays *The Dyer's Hand*, W. H. Auden discusses this problem: "It is both the glory and the shame of poetry that its medium is not its private property, that a poet cannot invent his words and that words are products, not of nature, but of a human society which uses them for a thousand different purposes. In modern societies where language is continually being debased and reduced to nonspeech, the poet is in constant danger of having his ear corrupted. . . ." Isabella Gardner has easily avoided that corruption, though she has surely felt her language pulled in contrary directions by the personal significance and emotion she attaches to the words she selects and arranges in poems, and by the limiting definitions and standards—to say nothing of deflations and perversions—imposed on them in society-at-large. Her poetry attains its distinctive quality by the conjunction of lyricism with a penetrating vision of life.

The poem "At the Zoo" demonstrates Miss Gardner's imaginative activity with all restraints cast aside. Though it is ostensibly a poem of at least partial lamentation, an infectious mood of joy and boundless energy dominates it from beginning to end. The poet starts by lodging her fundamental complaint against the loss of colorful mythological creatures who once captured man's fancy but now exist only in memory—presumably the memory of poets alone. Next she expresses in a lively way her devotion to various members of the animal kingdom, an affection

quite plain in other poems as well; but her enthusiasm is
dampened because these creatures are imprisoned in their
zoos. The fourth, and last, stanza proposes freedom and
renewal, a kind of paradisaical image, which begins with
the creatures already named at the poem's outset but now,
through its emotional resonance, tries to implicate everything in its burst of new life:

O the phoenix is gone and the unicorn
and the Chinese Nightingale.
No White Whale blows
nor Persian rose,
the buffalo is robe and dust.

I have a headlong leaping lust
for zig and zag and hues and cries,
for the paradox of the musky ox
and the mute giraffe's embarrassed eyes.

One should not (in this zoo) throw down a glove.
It is the bars that shame a zebra out of love
and flinch the tender faces of giraffes
who stick their necks out and are good for laughs.
The beautiful the gentle the enraged
the strange the pitiful are shooed and caged
the preying cats and the shy kine who browse
on treetops. Peanuts are not thrown to cows.

If the buffalo quicken in his hide
and the phoenix rise and the virgin bride
lie with the unicorn
Roland's horn and Omar's rose and Moby Dick
    will blow
and every piper will be pied and cages will be
    never,

giraffes will wink and zebras prink and spring come
    on forever.

This last stanza works toward a remarkable rhythmical
climax, analogous to its meaning, which builds up through
lines of moderate length and then through unusually long
ones. Miss Gardner exhibits here and elsewhere great skill
in manipulating with so much ease lengthy lines that
ordinarily might be cumbersome and wooden. The rhythmical climax is also the high point of her vision, reflecting
an attitude of compassion for captive life that is characteristic of her fundamental assertion of liberty and regenera-
tion. In "To Thoreau on Rereading Walden" she praises
that writer for his "taut and tender gaze" at "herds of
birds and fishes, stars in droves," but nevertheless un-
covers in him a terrible lack, a narrowness of love:

> You loved the faces in the fire, Thoreau,
> the goldgreen pickerel, the huddling snow.
> I too love these, and O love you, fierceheart,
> and yet were you, like Lazarus, to rise,
> you would look everywhere but in my eyes.

Thoreau stands accused in her mind of a failure to seek
or win any human love, and in the final line is seen to
have "dried safely" in his "shroud" as a result. The poet's
censure is, of course, not total; she loves what he loved
but knows her emotion must go further. Isolation is no
virtue in Miss Gardner's poetry, which constantly puts
before us the imagery of relationships, the patterns of
sympathy and understanding.

Prominence is given to the question of relationships at
the very beginning of *Birthdays from the Ocean* in the
form of an introductory poem called "That 'Craning of
the Neck'" and two quotations from the Jewish philosopher Martin Buber, one of which is an epigraph to the
book, the other an epigraph to the poem. The first epi-

graph provides the title for the introductory poem and may have been the inspiration for it:

> Believe in the simple magic of life, in service in the universe, and the meaning of that waiting, that alertness, that "craning of the neck" in creatures will dawn upon you.

This brief but amazing piece of advice is really accepted by Miss Gardner as more than an epigraph or the source of a poem's title; it serves her as a moral and artistic credo. This poet is in her work "a conjurer, a believer," as Richard Eberhart says; and her poems are "in service in the universe" as celebration and commemoration of the mysterious variety and beauty of life in its changing but recurring moments. And so Miss Gardner commits herself poetically to a complicated network of relations with the living cosmos.

One of the finest formulations of this commitment in both theme and the actual substance and texture of the writing occurs in her poem "Of Flesh and Bone." Here again are many of the long, opulent lines we have already mentioned. The poem gets underway in childhood recollections which first affirm the amplitude of human existence and next adopt a steadfast rejection of death:

> Child and girl each morning summer winter or dismay my eyes saw waterfalls my ears heard madrigals
> I tasted strawberries touched moss smelt hay and roses, and through the blue
> the bright sky I with my first and once-love flew.
> Willow-boned sun-marrowed and air-skinned,
> sea-water in my veins, I drank wine and the southwest wind.
> The noun death and the verb to die were exiled from my vocabulary, and when the salty boys and sunburned girls I

mooned with on the honeysuckled porch through
     locust-
loud and sigh-soft summer nights did speculate
     upon the disposition of my dust
I said to them I am a girl of flesh and bone, my
     shift's no shroud,
and d-e-a-t-h is the word I do not say out loud.
That is the word I said that I will not admit.

While the others assume the usual adolescent postures
that declare a wish to die young, the poet, like Yeats in
"A Dialogue of Self and Soul," would be "content to live
it all again/And yet again":

I vowed that eyeless earless, loinless lonely,
I would refuse to die; that even if only
one sense was left me, touch or smell or taste,
I would choose to live; that in a sewer of waste
a thicket of pain a mountain of fear or the sea-
wrack of sorrow I would beg, steal, and betray to be.

Her girlhood fear of death, she goes on to say, was of
"the releasing/of the I," the loss of self-identity, rather
than by any terror of pain or suffering. As she matured
her anxiety shifted to the anticipation of an "engagement
[with death] some tomorrow." What she is so reluctant to
abandon is her selfhood and, through it, her communion
with the abundance of the world. The unknown element
in death which most irritates her is, understandably, the
time of its arrival, for one is forced by this uncertainty always to keep the end in mind. In the closing stanza Miss
Gardner returns momentarily to the pleasures of living,
asserts a desire to appoint the hour of her own death so
as to escape the annoyance of expectation, and, at the last,
restates her basic attachment to her human, earthly nature. So strong is that tie that she can envisage herself
watching death face to face as it comes to claim her from

within. Though this image is "dead-certain" and the poet's "horror," that very fact sustains the special value she has placed on her life in opposition to the threat of a "coming nothingness":

> Now mornings are still miracles and my dear now-
> love is my true
> love and we fly we fly. . .O the sky was never
> once so bright and blue
> and I still wish to live with living's theft-
> ing and assault if even one sense will be left,
> but to escape the meals and miles of waiting
> I might elect the hour of my negating
> and sleep peacefully to death some winter night,
> cold finally to morning and to mourners and to
> fright.
> Still, flesh and bone is wilful, and this knowledge
> is dead-certain and my horror,
> that I shall not close my eyes when ITS eyes stare
> out of mine in every mirror.

The hidden fears and hesitancies we nourish in ourselves in a twisted effort to avoid encounters with the multifarious realities of the universe we inhabit are taken by Miss Gardner as the theme of another poem, "The Panic Vine." Botanical and biological details in the imagery suggest the primary character of this psychic malady which so ruthlessly circumscribes our outer existence too. But these details lead on to others that hint at something like, if not exactly the same as, the exposure of the psyche's secrets during the course of psychoanalysis. It is, however, a sort of auto-analysis the poet recommends; its goal is not simply a more durable self but also, once more, that attitude of openness to creation which unveils an otherwise neglected dimension of all human experience:

The panic vine quickens on the spine with the rise
and fall of every breath; and blooms inside the
eyes.
A cold fruit bulges from the veins of wrists and
arms
to bleed a virus juice into our sueded palms.
We spread disease when our be-gloved infrequent
rites
of greeting are performed. If we exhume the roots
that lie in nightsoil bedded with the lungs of crows
roots watered by the coiled insistent garden hose
cold-framed against the thorn the analytic wind
the dazzling showers of the thundering sun bird
blood
the grey goose feather and the white mare-mother's
cud—
if we expose these roots to weather and to wound
they would survive and we could bear the scattered
rose
the spattered foal the honking flight and the sun's
alms.

Miss Gardner's second collection, *The Looking Glass*
(1961), reveals no particular alteration in her outlook.
Though it contains some of her lightest verse—especially
in "Saloon Suite," "Canzonetta," and "Summers Ago"—
the book also includes several elegies; in spite of the airi-
ness of the pieces just mentioned, a vein of seriousness is
apparent. The best of the elegies, I believe, is the one
addressed to Dr. Louis Cholden and called, in the Yiddish
phrase which means "farewell," "Zei Gesund." This poem
does not deviate from the positive humanistic vision already indicated in the previous work; the dead man who
is honored here is a person whose "life-spirit" was "robust
past compare." As a medical man and a psychiatrist he
had healed the sick and restored them to life. For himself, he did not fear death and came to accept it when he

was confronted with the impossibility of recovery. So, Miss Gardner maintains, it is we, the living, who grieve at the loss of this man to ourselves; we do not mourn his suffering but our own deprivation. In "Of Flesh and Bone" the poet states her religious convictions, such as they are: "I am not faith-less but with those who see no future in eternity I do agree." Thus we find that her testimony to the deceased doctor's survival is kept within the mortal terms of those who will remember him and receive guidance from his example:

> It is not easy to remember that you died.
> Neither your funeral nor our tears persuade
> us, yet, that you have died. We shall confide
> to you in phantasy through years of need
> the flabby failure, shabby sin, and pride-
> fully, the high Hungarian deed.
> Our spirits shall by your quick soul be fed
> until our bodies, too, are dead.

Personal though her elegies and other poems in the book, such as "Nightmare" and the extremely moving "Widow's Yard" may be, the piece that gives its title to the entire collection is one of the most revealing, as well as one of the most fully achieved, to be found there. A type of stoicism, reminiscent of certain of the Elizabethan lyricists, is manifest in "Zei Gesund," and another version of it becomes apparent in "On Looking in the Looking Glass." Miss Gardner describes in this poem a pitiless inspection of her face in the mirror; her close and unsparing eye reads every line, interprets it; opens up past, present, and future to investigation; bares secret worries and inner deficiencies. A diversity of selves is laid bare and brought to consciousness and to the order of language, just as in this strange little colloquy of the interior life by Paul Valéry two apparently different voices below the mind's surface contribute to the poet's total self:

—Who is there?
—I.
—Who is I?
—Thou.
And that is the awakening—the Thou and the I.

In "On Looking in the Looking Glass," as in her other
poems from the more recent volume that strike a grave
note, Miss Gardner exercises a new economy and restraint
in diction and music to control nearly overpowering effects. Since those effects are weakened by piecemeal quotation, I give the poem here in its entirety:

Your small embattled eyes dispute a face
that middle-aging sags and creases.
Besieged, your eyes protest and plead,
your wild little eyes are bright, and bleed.

And now in an instant's blink my stare
seizes in your beleaguered glare
the pristine gaze the blown-glass stance
of your once
total innocence.
I see and dare the child you were.

And for a wink's lasting, There
Now in your blistered eyes dazzles the flare
of Youth with years and love to swear
the kindling enkindled fire
heedless and sheer . . .
I see and fear the girl you were.

And now for a tic's lending, Now for the stint
of a second's fission I light to the glint
of your Daemon, that familiar whom you stint
so prodigally. Shunting, shan't-
ing, wincing fabricant

I see the maker that you want
and aren't.

And now just now I closed your eyes
your infant ancient naked eyes.
Gaze glare and flare and glint are buried by
my neutral eye-
lids. These island citadels are now surrendered
and with imagination's eye I see you dead.

Of course, Miss Gardner's fundamental wordplay has
not disappeared in this poem, but it has been subordi-
nated to her total vision. As the intensity of that vision
increases with the progression of the poem toward considerations of her artistic vocation and the intuition of
her own death, the language, in the second half of the
fourth stanza, begins to loosen under the pressure of pent-
up emotions.

It would be presumptuous to attempt a prediction
of Miss Gardner's future poetry, but it appears as if the
exuberance of *Birthdays from the Ocean* had been perma-
nently tempered and controlled by more sober concerns.
Her recent tendency is to make her language work for an
experience, except in poems that are quite clearly no more
than light exercises. The earlier poems often exist in part
as experiences generated primarily by words, but Miss
Gardner's newer poetry, while it shows no loss of linguistic power, embodies a deepening of insight and a firmer
grounding of her attitudes. Her two distinguished books
enable us to acquaint ourselves with the line of development of her truly lyrical art.

VIII

Robert Lowell

"In a young man like Lowell, whether we like his Catholicism or not," wrote Allen Tate in his brief introduction to *Land of Unlikeness* (1944), "there is at least a memory of the spiritual dignity of man, now sacrificed to mere secularization and a craving for mechanical order." This first book by Lowell, unsuccessful as it is in certain ways, immediately sets forth the dramatic tension implied by the opposing forces of spirituality and secularism Tate mentions. Visible in language and style, as well as in theme, that tension has come to seem characteristic of a sizable portion of Lowell's work; not until the publication of *Life Studies* (1959) did his work show thoroughgoing changes. While the tension of the early poetry is religious in nature, we should not think of it as either wholly objective or institutional and doctrinal. The religious viewpoint in Lowell's writing is a means of dramatizing the poet's subjective attitudes and his emotions. In saying this I do not, of course, intend either to disparage Lowell's religious convictions or to question their sincerity. One cannot read these poems without feeling at once the genuine and substantial nature of his beliefs. I do think, though, that the objective framework of most of the poems—that is, the antagonism of Catholicism toward New England Calvinism and the Protestant ethic—masks the author's very personal involvement in the matters that go to make them up. The outrage, the violent attacks occupying so much of *Land of Unlikeness*, are less those of a prophet provoked to lofty condemnation by the unbearable corruption of civilization than they are the result of the poet's awareness, harsh and frustrating, that he too has emerged from the same tainted circumstance. His sometimes unfocused and excessively vindictive criticism of moral failure and of spiritual lassitude appear now to have been partially some kind of purgation for the poet as well—perhaps an effort, through the cold fury of his art, to free himself once and for all of an inheritance he had already abandoned by will and intellect.

Robert Lowell comes from the distinguished New England family that counts among its members James Russell Lowell and Amy Lowell. He was raised in Boston and has pictured some of his childhood in his poetry and in his brilliant autobiographical narrative in prose, "91 Revere Street," which likewise provides detailed portraits of his mother and father during a specific period in their lives. As Hugh B. Staples writes in his excellent study, *Robert Lowell: The First Twenty Years*, to which I am much indebted, "to understand his development as a poet, we have to see . . . Lowell's sense of antagonism to [this] order of things." His rebelliousness took the form of a conversion to Roman Catholicism and the employment of its theology and symbolism to combat his local and historical descent, the religion and morality of his forefathers. *Lord Weary's Castle* (1946), which is an amazing creative leap ahead of the first book and which won Lowell the Pulitzer Prize, makes more explicit the personal nature of the poet's rejections and his beliefs. Though only one poem in *Land of Unlikeness* (later reprinted in *Lord Weary's Castle*)—"In Memory of Arthur Winslow"—draws its material from Lowell's family his-

tory, several in his second volume plainly deal with such
subjects and several more exhibit Lowell the man as the
meditative speaker who stands at their center. *The Mills
of the Kavanaughs* (1951) moves away from the author's
biography and relies solely on fictional narrators for its
dramatic monologues, but Lowell returns to his family
and to himself with greater frankness and absence of restraint in *Life Studies*.

Lowell is conscious of history as it comes to a point of
concentration in himself and as he fights against the tradition to which he has fallen heir. In addition, we know, as
John McCormick tells us in an interview with Lowell
(*Poetry*, January 1953), that this poet is further conscious
of history through his wide reading in it. Looking at his
New England heritage from the older and more European position of his Catholicism, he not only judges that
heritage and finds it wanting but tries to allay its ghosts
which torment him. In the opening section of "The First
Sunday in Lent" Lowell imagines himself a child once
again, watching from the attic window of his house the
crowds of worshippers on their way home from church
services. The beginning of the first stanza specifies his
outlook and enforces a spiritual as well as a physical distance from those he views ("A world below my window"). The experience here is clearly one in which the
mind of the mature poet invades the body of his boyhood:

> The crooked family chestnut sighs, for March,
> Time's fool, is storming up and down the town;
> The gray snow squelches and the well-born stamp
> From sermons in a scolded, sober mob
> That wears away the Sabbath with a frown,
> A world below my window.

The chestnut tree's crookedness indicates a warp extending beyond the immediate boundaries of family to
include the churchgoers, for whom Lent apparently will

bring neither repentence nor humility, breeding instead
that "frown" which implies indignation and perhaps a
self-righteous wrath. However, the poet, in the manner
of the child he evokes, abruptly switches his attention
from the crowd outside to the articles that have gathered
over the years in this attic storage room. The collection of
objects calls from his memory fragments of history; and
his enumeration of these accumulated objects has its indirect bearing on the throng below, for the churchgoers,
and the poet too, issue from that history:

> This is the fifth floor attic where I hid
> My stolen agates and the cannister
> Preserved from Bunker Hill—feathers and guns,
> Matchlock and flintlock and percussion-cap;
> Gettysburg etched upon the cylinder
> Of Father's Colt. A Lüger of a Hun,
> Once blue as Satan, breaks Napoleon,
> My china pitcher. Cartridge boxes trap
> A chipmunk on the saber where they slid.

Weapons form a record of the triumphant history and
tradition of the worshippers, and allusion to the Civil
War may revive memories of the defeat of a largely
agrarian society by the North, with its commercial and industrial interests. Behind the pursuit of "progress"—
which Lowell heartily despises—lies much of the ascetic
zeal of Protestant New England. Though the people dispersing after church might smugly, but gravely, assume
God is with them, the poet believes otherwise; and in
the concluding stanza the doom that fell upon pagan
Troy when "the populous/Shrines held carnival" is
sharply juxtaposed with the fate of these modern puritans
who "burrow into the lion's mouth to die." Yet out of
this destruction there arrives the possibility of renewal
through grace. The "unblemished Adam" for whom the
poet prays, reborn from this "lust and dust," will see:

The limbs of the tormented chestnut tree
Tingle, and hear the March-winds lift and cry:
"The Lord of Hosts will overshadow us."

In this instance the tree may be intended to represent
the Tree of Knowledge, therefore a symbol of human
guilt, and also the tree upon which Christ redeemed man
(an old Christian legend claims the wood of the Cross is
cut from the Tree of Knowledge). In any event, both
guilt and expiation come together in these lines.

It can be said without exaggeration that the predominant mood in *Lord Weary's Castle* is negative. Human
life is consistently viewed with regard to its outcome in
death; and Lowell does not spare the reader any tough
realism of detail, as a couple of selected passages should
be sufficient to demonstrate:

> This Easter, Arthur Winslow, less than dead,
> Your people set you up in Phillips' House
> To settle off your wrestling with the crab—
> The claws drop flesh upon your yachting blouse
> Until longshoreman Charon come and stab
> Through your adjusted bed
> And crush the crab.
>
>   ("In Memory of Arthur Winslow")

>   Here my father saw
> The leadman trip against a pigpen, crash,
> Legs spread, his codpiece split, his fiddle
>   smash . . .
> These mammoth vintners danced their blood out
>   in the straw.
>
>   ("The Blind Leading the Blind")

Mortality is, of course, in Christian belief the condition
of things as a result of the Fall, but in Lowell's poetry it
seems sometimes to be almost equivalent to damnation,
though, as we shall see, this interpretation must be quali-

fied. One of his persistent images is that of Charon—as
in the first quotation above—the figure from Greek mythology whose task it is to ferry the souls of the dead across
the river Styx or the river Acheron into the underworld.
Lowell's Charon is, appropriately, a grim being, frequently a figure for death itself, and he carries ominous
suggestions of hell when he appears—as if, that is to say,
the fate of a soul were very nearly predetermined. Curiously, this is a feeling or impression the reader may get,
and not necessarily what actually happens. The general
atmosphere of many of the poems also creates this impression, but the sudden intervention of God or Christ,
or the request for such an intervention (they may amount
to the same thing, dramatically speaking) abolishes the
atmosphere of hopelessness and utter loss by introducing
the possibility of the miraculous or of salvation. Randall
Jarrell understands this, as he does other movements in
Lowell's verse, to be a release from confinement to openness and freedom.

Let us look at an example of this divine intrusion
which promises relief to a condition of life that is otherwise bleak and somber. "Colloquy in Black Rock," one
of Lowell's most fully achieved and deservedly celebrated
poems, begins in a definite location (Black Rock, a section of Bridgeport, Connecticut, a city in which he lived
for a period during World War II) as a dialogue between
the poet and his heart. This dialogue closely resembles
an old convention of Christian and other philosophical
poetry—the dialogue between body and soul. Andrew
Marvell's poem of that title is a good representative of
the type, and so is Yeats' "A Dialogue of Self and Soul."
It is only natural in such a poetic circumstance that the
theme should be related to man's mortality, to the inevitability of death. We ought to notice at once the connection between the pounding, vibrating jack-hammer
(which also depicts the geographical shape of Black Rock
jutting out into the ocean) and the racing heart of the

poet. His heartbeats, sounding ever faster and syncopated
like jazz music, bring him always closer to death. Hop-
kinsian diction and energetic rhythms add to the rapid
effects, exerting pressure against the order of rhyme and
meter; the result is a very forceful poetic statement:

> Here the jack-hammer jabs into the ocean;
> My heart, you race and stagger and demand
> More blood-gangs for your nigger-brass percussions,
> Till I, the stunned machine of your devotion,
> Clanging upon this cymbal of a hand,
> Am rattled screw and footloose. All discussions
>
> End in the mud-flat detritus of death.
> My heart, beat faster, faster. In Black Mud
> Hungarian workmen give their blood
> For the martyre Stephen, who was stoned to death.

Just as the jack-hammer can reduce solid matter to a
pulp, so the driving tempo of the heart urges human life
toward its finish. In the second stanza these analogies are
continued in the figures of the Hungarian workmen, who,
we imagine, are working feverishly during wartime, and
in the person of St. Stephen the martyr, who predicts
Christ's appearance in the fourth stanza and the theme
of Corpus Christi. Mud and dust engage the poet's imagination in stanza three as he envisages various things
coming to their end. The final part of this stanza leads
him to knowledge of his own death: "the dust" on his
heart will ultimately turn to the same ugly mud that
envelops everything:

> Black Mud, a name to conjure with: O mud
> For watermelons gutted to the crust,
> Mud for the mole-tide harbor, mud for mouse,
> Mud for the armored Diesel fishing tubs that thud
> A year and a day to wind and tide; the dust
> Is on this skipping heart that shakes my house . . .

The sentence Lowell has started here does not conclude with this stanza but with the first line of the next one, a line that completely switches about the mood of the poem by means of a sudden and unexpected identification of the poet's body with the human form that Christ assumed in the mystery of His incarnation (the significance of Corpus Christi). Thus the religious theme hits with its full impact when we think of Christ taking on human flesh and suffering its mortal term in order to salvage man from its wreckage. Both Christ and St. Stephen "ransom" him—though in very different degrees —through the sacrifice of their lives:

> House of our Savior who was hanged till death.
> My heart, beat faster, faster. In Black Mud
> Stephen the martyre was broken down to blood:
> Our ransom is the rubble of his death.

Finally, the poem's last stanza completes the reversal of mood begun in the preceding one. Christ appears, walking on the black ocean waters already seen at the outset of the poem. Then, in the image of the kingfisher which is often used to symbolize Him, He—the bewilderment of the world—enters the mud, the "rubble" of our decaying mortal flesh, to bring renewal and to awaken the life of the spirit (the fire and bird link this image with the Holy Ghost too):

> Christ walks on the black water. In Black Mud
> Darts the kingfisher. On Corpus Christi, heart,
> Over the drum-beat of St. Stephen's choir
> I hear him, *Stupor Mundi*, and the mud
> Flies from his hunching wings and beak—my
>   heart,
> The blue kingfisher dives on you in fire.

The same miraculous intervention is hoped for in the powerful elegy for Lowell's cousin, Warren Winslow, "dead at sea." In this poem, "The Quaker Graveyard in

Nantucket," the poet turns after five sections of meditation on violence, death, and human folly to an interlude of calm reflectiveness. Into the elegy as a whole Lowell has worked echoes from Melville of Ahab's mad pursuit of Moby Dick, as well as a description of a drowned man from Thoreau's *Cape Cod*. More than a mourning of Warren Winslow's loss, this poem, like "Lycidas" and "Adonais" with which it has been compared, develops themes related to or arising from the occasion. Lowell's choice of epigraph from the Book of Genesis becomes, as the poem progresses, an ironical commentary on the men of New England: "Let men have dominion over the fishes of the sea and the fowls of the air and the beasts and the whole earth, and every creeping creature upon the earth." We are shown the awful abuse of this privilege by greedy and cruel Quaker whalers in part V. There the poet is speaker; and as the violent horror of the chase and kill of the whale moves to its climax, his is the voice that cries out to Christ to absorb the evil men commit. The passage exemplifies Lowell's tremendous gift for overwhelmingly graphic description that still carries a symbolic weight; his sense of sound and his compelling rhythm bring it alive:

> When the whale's viscera go and the roll
> Of its corruption overruns this world
> Beyond tree-swept Nantucket and Wood's Hole
> And Martha's Vineyard, Sailor, will your sword
> Whistle and fall and sink into the fat?
> In the great ash-pit of Jehosaphat
> The bones cry for the blood of the white whale,
> The fat flukes arch and whack about its ears,
> The death-lance churns into the sanctuary, tears
> The gun-blue swingle, heaving like a flail,
> And hacks the coiling life out: it works and drags
> And rips the sperm-whale's midriff into rags,
> Gobbets of blubber spill to wind and weather,

Sailor, and gulls go around the stoven timbers
Where the morning stars sing out together
And thunder shakes the white surf and dismembers
The red flag hammered in the mast head. Hide,
Our steel, Jonas Messias, in Thy side.

Christ, whose side was pierced by a Roman soldier's
spear as He lay dying on the cross, and Jonah, whose
three-day captivity inside a whale before being spewed
up was read by Biblical exegetes as a prophetic allegory
of Jesus' death, burial, and resurrection, join together in
the poet's mind as he calls for divine assistance. Section
VI, "Our Lady of Walsingham," if it does not supply us
with the vision of Christ's redeeming gesture we found in
"Colloquy in Black Rock," at least points in a similar
direction.

Lowell lifts some of the details of the shrine in Walsingham (England) from E. I. Watkin's *Catholic Art and
Culture* but turns them, of course, to his own purpose.
This section contrasts with earlier parts and with the final
one that follows. Opening with an account of the peni-
tents who, by custom, removed their shoes and walked
barefoot to the shrine, the first of the two stanzas goes
on to describe the quiet beauty of the English countryside surrounding it. But with the second stanza interest
changes from the pleasant qualities of this world to the
austere other-worldliness evident in the Virgin's con-
templative pose:

There's no comeliness
At all or charm in that expressionless
Face with its heavy eyelids. As before,
This face, for centuries a memory,
Non est species, neque decor,
Expressionless, expresses God: it goes
Past castled Sion. She knows what God knows,
Not Calvary's Cross nor crib at Bethlehem
Now, and the world shall come to Walsingham.

The eyes of Our Lady, like those of the supernatural
figures which so fascinated Yeats, turn inward or away
from earthly reality and seem to be attentive to a transcendent plane of being. Though she has known the human experience in an extreme way ("Calvary's Cross
. . . crib at Bethlehem") through her son's life, the Virgin is not placed here beside the Walsingham altar
merely to gaze with approval on her pastoral setting as
if it were the City of God ("Sion"); her pose underlines
a state more rigorous and absolute, and one not so readily
attained. The last line clarifies her mediating function
between earth and heaven—(see part IV, "A Prayer for
My Grandfather to Our Lady," for a specific example of
this)—and so she too serves as a means of undoing the
hard determinacy of existence.

In such poems as "The Drunken Fisherman," "The
Death of the Sheriff," "At the Indian Killer's Grave," and
"Between the Porch and the Altar" Lowell further portrays the chaos of contemporary life, burdened with the
past and spiritually empty. Some of these poems are fictional narratives or monologues with fictional speakers—
though, as Randall Jarrell says, all the voices sound like
Robert Lowell's—and in this respect they look forward
to the poems of *The Mills of the Kavanaughs*. Fictional
speakers and narratives are not, I think, this poet's *forte*,
but exceptions must be made. One of them is "Adam
and Eve," section II of "Between the Porch and the
Altar," a slightly confusing poem about adultery. Here
Lowell vividly sets against one another images of the
New England farmer—enshrined in the statue of the
Concord Minute Man—and two illicit lovers of the present day: each is corroded by the internal workings of lust
partially fostered by a tradition of life and the moral
character of a society. The farmer "sizzles on his shaft
all day," and even this statue might be "melting down
like sculptured lard" in the narrator's near hallucinatory
vision, brought on by his internal storm of passion and

guilt. He decides that "Never to have lived is best;/Man
tasted Eve with death." Now nothing can avoid the taint
of moral corruption:

> What is exempt?
> I eye the statue with an awed contempt
> And see the puritanical façade
> Of the white church that Irish exiles made
> For Patrick—that Colonial from Rome
> Had magicked the charmed serpents from their
>   home,
> As though he were the Piper. Will his breath
> Scorch the red dragon of my nerves to death?

Obviously it is the "red dragon" of the narrator-adult-
erer's "nerves" that explains the agonized feeling of the
stanza. Inner tension resulting from pangs of conscience
causes him to envisage the social and religious background of his actions in startling fashion. He looks at a
Catholic church and thinks of it as dyed with a streak of
puritanism too. At this point the narrative moves outward
from the man's thoughts to his relations with his mistress
and his "cold-eyed seedy fathers" who "threw their lives
away" in search of success and respectability: "Sterile,
forbidding nameplates on the bricks/Above a kettle."
Finally, at the end of the poem, the snakes driven from
Ireland by the powerful St. Patrick reappear as disguises
for Satan, symbolizing both sexuality and the choice of
sin. The concluding scene is one of terror and judgment:

> You cry for help. Your market basket rolls
> With all its baking apples in the lake.
> You watch the whorish slither of a snake
> That chokes a duckling. When we try to kiss,
> Our eyes are slits and cringing, and we hiss;
> Scales glitter on our bodies as we fall.
> The farmer melts upon his pedestal.

After the primordial Fall in Eden, the fateful act of defection is continually repeated throughout history. The legacy of a puritan ancestry is insufficient defense against the temptations of the serpent; and as the lovers fall the idol of their culture, the sturdy and protective Minute Man, melts away in the heat of their passion. In a few poems, notably "As a Plane Tree by the Water" and "Where the Rainbow Ends," Lowell carries his poetic vision to the level of prophecy, disclosing images of a society passing through its last stages and trembling on the brink of apocalypse. Such a vision corresponds to that of many of Lowell's predecessors among modern writers; Eliot, Yeats, Lawrence, Auden, Kunitz, and others frequently exhibit a similar outlook.

The Mills of the Kavanaughs marks the last phase of Lowell's earlier manner and, simultaneously, prefigures some of his new work. Its seven poems are all monologues, with the title poem the longest and most ambitious—though not the best—of them. In it Anne Kavanaugh, the young widow of a Naval officer who has committed suicide, sits in the garden of their Maine home near his grave and plays solitaire with the husband's Catholic family Bible as her imaginary opponent. The poem consists of her conscious thoughts and observations about herself, her husband, and their lives, but her mind also drifts into daydream and revery, where she recalls her childhood (the Kavanaughs had adopted her as a child, so that she married their son, with whom she had grown up). These changeable currents of her mind create certain difficulties for one who seeks a strict narrative to follow, and the structure is further complicated by an intricate and sometimes artificial use of mythical allusion, which is discussed in careful detail in Hugh Staples' book. A statue of Persephone, goddess of the underworld, stands in the Kavanaugh garden, and in her musing Anne identifies herself with this mythical female and so reveals, as Staples indicates, her own death wish. Her husband becomes Pluto, lord of the Underworld, in the same mythological scheme; and on yet another level they play the roles of Narcissus and Echo.

In spite of remarkable passages the poem seems often to protract Lowell's familiar devices of compression and allusion beyond the requirements of the work. However, we can see evidence throughout the book of his growing interest in the study of individual persons. One of the annoying features of the title poem is the repetition of characteristic sound patterns: run-on lines with their insistent rhyming that conclude abruptly in the middle of another line prevent naturalness of speech and tend to create turbulent or choppy effects. Yet much of the detail is magnificently rendered, and there are sections, like the closing lines, rich in music and meaning. Here, at last, Anne Kavanaugh merges her fate with Persephone's, and submits her will to her dead husband:

> "Why must we mistrust
> Ourselves with Death who takes the world on trust?
> Although God's brother, and himself a god,
> Death whipped his horses through the startled sod;
> For neither conscience nor omniscience warned
> Him from his folly, when the virgin scorned
> His courtship, and the quaking earth revealed
> Death's desperation to the Thracian field.
> And yet we think the virgin took no harm:
> She gave herself because her blood was warm—
> And for no other reason, Love, I gave
> Whatever brought me gladness to the grave."

Of the other poems, "David and Bathsheba in the Public Garden" falls into sheer confusion, and "Thanksgiving's Over" is contrived and overcharged with melodrama. Critics have remarked the absence of religious elements in these poems. Though one still finds Catholic

materials in use—particularly in the title poem, in
"Thanksgiving's Over," and in "Mother Marie Thérèse"
—they are simply materials like any others; the fierce
metaphysical vision is gone. The finest poem in the collection, "Mother Marie Thérèse," is the monologue of a
Canadian nun lamenting the past days of Maris Stella
House under the rule of a now dead Mother Superior,
Marie Thérèse, a worldly-wise woman who delighted in
possessions, in secular knowledge and personal pleasures.
What Lowell might well have judged severely before he
now shows fascination for; the dead nun is drawn with
the loving care a fine fiction writer, a Chekhov or the
early Joyce, would lavish on a favorite character, and with
a poet's economy:

> Like Proserpina, who fell
> Six months a year from earth to flower in hell;
> She half renounced by Candle, Book and Bell
> Her flowers and fowling pieces for the Church.
> She never spared the child and spoiled the birch;
> And how she'd chide her novices, and pluck
> Them by the ears for gabbling in Canuck,
> While she was reading Rabelais from her chaise,
> Or parroting the *Action Française*.

At first glance, *Life Studies* may appear to constitute a
complete break with Lowell's previous work. Except for
"Beyond the Alps" and a detail or two in "Waking in the
Blue," the new poems bear no traces of Catholic beliefs;
and the baroque mannerism and the iambics of the early
poetry have been replaced by a calmer, more reflective
style which employs, in many instances, free verse or very
irregular lines. Individual persons—Ford Madox Ford,
Santayana, Hart Crane—the Lowell family, and the
poet's own life as a child and a man provide the subjects
for these poems. Along with them is printed the prose
narrative, "91 Revere Street," which acts as an introduction and a supplement to the "Life Studies." Yet these

changes do not wholly divorce Lowell from his past writing. We have already said that the dramatic monologues of *Lord Weary's Castle* and, particularly, of *The Mills of the Kavanaughs* prepare for such alterations; and Lowell eases us into this latest phase with an opening section of four poems reminiscent of his earlier poetry.

The first and most important of these poems is "Beyond the Alps," which maintains its author's usual concern with history, morality, and religion, but in a more relaxed way. The "I" of the narrator is unmistakably Lowell himself. He is riding the train from Rome to Paris in 1950, "the year Pius XII defined the dogma of Mary's bodily assumption." As the train climbs into "fallow Alpine snow," he reflects on the meaning of where he has been and where he is going. Thoughts of his own situation weave in and out of thoughts about contemporary events, about civilization past and present: "Life changed to landscape." His departure from Rome was reluctant and brings to mind the fallen Mussolini ("He was one of us/only, pure prose") and then the mode of life enjoyed by the poet's wealthy predecessors in the nineteenth century:

> I envy the conspicuous
> waste of our grandparents on their grand tours—
> long-haired Victorian sages accepted the universe,
> while breezing on their trust funds through the
> world.

Very evidently Lowell does not share the same leisure or frame of mind. Differing views of the universe—again initiated by Rome, this time in its religious character—turn up in the next stanza, where the declaration at the Vatican of the Virgin Mary's Assumption is dramatized. Lowell implies that the "crowds" outside St. Peter's calling for the Pope are ignorant of the proclamation's significance, and that, as Hugh Staples says, their enthusiasm is directed instead toward the Catholic vicar as an earthly leader. Certainly the poet's attitude here is ironic and skeptical, distant from his previous adherence to the Church. The Pope is shown with an instrument of modern technology in one hand and a tame bird perched on the other. Lowell perhaps suggests by this image that the Church has adjusted itself too nicely to the world of our time and has tamed the inspiration and efficacy of the Holy Ghost, often symbolized by a dove:

> When the Vatican made Mary's Assumption
>   dogma,
> the crowds at San Pietro screamed *Papa.*
> The Holy Father dropped his shaving glass,
> and listened. His electric razor purred,
> his pet canary chirped on his left hand.
> The lights of science couldn't hold a candle
> to Mary risen—at one miraculous stroke,
> angel-wing'd, gorgeous as a jungle bird!
> But who believed this? Who could understand?
> Pilgrims still kissed Saint Peter's brazen sandal.
> The Duce's lynched, bare, booted skull still spoke.
> God herded his people to the *coup de grâce*—
> the costumed Switzers sloped their pikes to push,
> O Pius, through the monstrous human crush. . . .

In his *Paris Review* interview with Frederick Seidel (reprinted in *Writers at Work, Second Series*) Lowell speaks of the fact that his later poems generally avoid religious symbolism and imagery: "in many ways [these poems] seem . . . more religious than the early ones, which are full of symbols and references to Christ and God." He does not believe his "experience [has] changed very much. It seems . . . clearer . . . now than it was then, but it's very much the same sort of thing that went into the religious poems—the same sort of struggle, light and darkness, the flux of experience. The morality seems much the same." Finally, Lowell says of his convictions, "you couldn't possibly say what creed I believed in. I've

wondered myself often." Nonetheless, the cool detachment and irony of "Beyond the Alps" signal the abandon-
ment of Catholic doctrine and symbolism in his art.
Dramatic tension, when we discover it, now exists between the poet as a person and society or some other
circumstance; it is no longer the product of a specifically
religious opposition. Lowell looks, it may be, a little en-
viously on those Victorian grandparents who could accept
the world as they found it; at any rate, he displays more
compassion and humanity in these poems. In a subsequent stanza, having "come to earth" again with the Alps
behind him, the poet looks back and considers the civilization of Greece, represented by the goddess Minerva.
But that civilization perished with its ideals, just as, he
seems to say, the Christian/Roman one is presently fail-
ing. The isolated couplet ending the poem offers no answers but thrusts at the poet the reality of his destination,
Paris, a center of modern life, which is also at the point
of collapse. The poem, like the moving train, reveals only
transience and change:

> Now Paris, our black classic, breaking up
> like killer kings on an Etruscan cup.

Throughout *Life Studies* Lowell falls back upon himself as an individual and withdraws from most external
forms of support. Yet if the poems tell us anything, they
tell us of the anguish of human weakness and vulnerability, the cost of private suffering. But the poems are victories over the pains and defeats of existence, and some
of them achieve a temporary evenness, a rather settled
view of experience that the earlier work, as is natural,
lacked. A fresh influence of William Carlos Williams,
whom Lowell has apparently long admired, and possibly
of W. D. Snodgrass, who was his student for a while,
enters his writing. Not only does the appearance of free
verse remind us of Williams, but also an increased attention to objects recalls the elder poet's ceaseless scru-

tiny of them. Snodgrass' poems, on the other hand, may have indicated to Lowell the possibilities latent in domestic and intimate themes. "Father's Bedroom" is simply a catalogue of things in that room, but they are carefully selected by the poet for description and become meaningful in terms of the book as a whole, as well as in themselves, because of what we learn about Commander Lowell from other poems and from "91 Revere Street." Like the other "Life Studies" this poem is a sketch, a lesser one to be sure, toward a canvas of finished portraits. We are not given the completed picture, however, since that would require fixing the figures rigidly and finally. With a novelist's shrewdness Lowell recognizes how he might easily destroy their fluid and ambiguous humanity —the source of their fascination for us. He maintains the same approach in his studies of the four writers. The sketch of Santayana, for example, covers his last days "at the monastery hospital," where the unrepentant old philosopher ("free-thinking Catholic infidel") kept at his writing in spite of the interruptions of visitors and the communal effort of the sisters to bring him back to the Church. The last lines pay tribute to Santayana's courage and tenacity of mind, and to the richness and wit of his books. Lowell has created a picture consciously emphasizing particular qualities of its subject that are not so remote from himself.

The poems about his family are, like the autobiographical narrative in prose, both compassionate and critical; and compassion would appear to win out, along with a natural but never overbearing family pride. All the same, he has not lost the sharp blade of judgment, nor has he at last succumbed to an order of life of which he disapproves. Lowell's wit still cuts to the quick:

Only teaching on Tuesdays, book-worming
in pajamas fresh from the washer each morning,
I hog a whole house on Boston's

> "hardly passionate Marlborough street,"
> where even the man
> scavenging filth in the back alley trash cans,
> has two children, a beach wagon, a helpmate,
> and is a "young Republican."
> ("Memories of West Street and Lepke")

Glimpses of Lowell's family piety as well as his rebel-
lious spirit are available in a poem such as "Grandparents." The beginning stanza relates his grandparents'
death as an initial fact—"They're altogether otherworldly
now"—and in a way that also closes off from the present
day the historical period they inhabited ("the nineteenth
century, tired of children, is gone"). Lowell can be readily identified as the poem's speaker, so that what we are
told comes to us through his memory, where his grandparents are caught forever in familiar poses, and through
his immediate perception:

> Back in my throw-away and shaggy span
> of adolescence, Grandpa still waves his stick
> like a policeman;
> Grandmother, like a Mohammedan, still wears her
>   thick
> lavender mourning and touring veil;
> the Pierce-Arrow clears its throat in a horse-stall.

The conclusion of the stanza echoes the famous poem by
the seventeenth-century mystical writer Henry Vaughan,
several lines of which apply to Lowell's own meditative
mood:

> They are all gone into the world of light;
>   And I alone sit lingering here!
> Their very memory is fair and bright,
>   And my sad thoughts doth clear.

The final portion of the passage from Vaughan, which
Lowell undoubtedly would like us to think of, separates
the past from the present that the poet inhabits. Lowell's

poem now leaves the images of his memory and turns to the situation as it is: he is visiting the Winslow farm he has inherited. That farm becomes the setting for the rest of the poem.

But memory again intrudes, for the return to the farm compares with a journey back to earlier years of his life. He roves through the house, inspecting one thing after another; each is attached to a life lived and revives it within him until he cries out with love and the pain of loss:

> The farm's my own!
> Back there alone,
> I keep indoors, and spoil another season.
> I hear the rattley little country gramophone
> racking its five foot horn:
> "O Summer Time!"
> Even at noon here the formidable
> *Ancien Régime* still keeps nature at a distance.
>   Five
> green shaded light bulbs spider the billiards-table;
> no field is greener than its cloth,
> where Grandpa, dipping sugar for us both,
> once spilled his demitasse.
> His favorite ball, the number three,
> still hides the coffee stain.
>
> Never again
> to walk there, chalk our cues,
> insist on shooting for us both.
> Grandpa! Have me, hold me, cherish me!
> Tears smut my fingers.

The agony here is, in its way, excruciating; Lowell's entry into the past through wakened memories not only reanimates the figure of his grandfather, for whom he has a special affection (see also "My Last Afternoon with Uncle Devereux Winslow"), but causes the poet to seek his childhood self as well. Yet he is still the adult too and so feels himself torn between these two selves—that is also, to repeat my descriptive terms, between the experience of love and the knowledge of loss. Abruptly, however, we are withdrawn from the regions of memory and planted firmly—and quite realistically—in the present once more. At the poem's finish we find Lowell performing a seemingly idle, whimsical gesture which, if it looks harmless, has yet a small sting of reversal about it. What he qualifies by it is more than the strong emotion for his grandfather and the past in which he has just indulged himself; he also qualifies the image of himself that he has given us in the poem. Through his slightly mischievous act we are compelled to realize the danger of trying to pin down this poet's complex artistic personality:

> There
> half my life-lease later,
> I hold an *Illustrated London News*—;
> disloyal still,
> I doodle handlebar
> mustaches on the last Russian Czar.

In the pictorial pages of an old issue of the conservative and patriotic *News* Lowell discovers the portrait of someone who, like his grandfather, stands for a now vanished mode of life that involved wealth, leisure, and class distinction. Though the poet was struck a few lines before by love and nostalgia, he does not accept his grandfather's world altogether; it is, after all, the world he rebelled against and grew away from. The doodled mustaches suddenly liberate him from the grip of memory and the emotions roused by it, and enable him to regain a perspective of distance and ironic detachment.

Following the poems about his grandparents and uncle, his mother and father, Lowell includes a series directly concerned with his own life. These pieces, with the exception of a short poem, " 'To Speak of the Woe That Is in Marriage,' " which is clearly not about the poet, make a concluding group for the book.

Most of the poems in this final group in *Life Studies* open onto the more intimate aspects of life, areas of experience that most of us would instinctively keep from public sight. In short, we are faced with a kind of confessional poetry. Lowell's marriage, his precarious mental state, his average day at a mental hospital, fragments of his wartime jail experience (he was sentenced as a conscientious objector)—these subjects enter his poetry. But Lowell is not alone among contemporary poets in his confessional tendencies. He has said that W. D. Snodgrass used private autobiographical material before him; and Snodgrass and Lowell have contributed heavily to the personal or intimate mood in much current American poetry. Any judgment of this highly personal disclosure must be founded on the meaningfulness of the artistic object created from it—that is to say, whether it can achieve the imaginative objectivity capable of establishing it as an independent and forceful work. Lowell does, I believe, accomplish this goal; and he grants us insight into the operations of a profound but restless and frightening spirit, which is frequently called upon to confront its own vertiginous instability:

> I myself am hell;
> nobody's here—
>   ("Skunk Hour")

Of the poets who grew up in the same period with Lowell only Theodore Roethke, Stanley Kunitz, and, very recently, John Berryman in his *77 Dream Songs* (1964) have stared so boldly into the mind's abysses, but they have done it without the emphasis on autobiographical accuracy of *Life Studies*.

"Waking in the Blue," a representative poem of the closing group, starts slowly and builds to a peak of tension by the end of the first stanza. Before we can be certain of our whereabouts in the poem, we see a university student who works as a "night attendant" awaking from sleep at a desk; then he "catwalks down our corridor." The possessive "our" places us at once with the first-person narrator—Lowell himself—and it is his response to the day and the environment that supplies the poem's substance. Lowell's own waking brings with it the gloomy realization of that environment (a mental hospital) and of his lonely captivity there. The passage describing his coming to consciousness wins much of its climactic strength through the change from a casual rhyme ("day"/"fairway") to a closer and more pronounced rhyming in the last three lines that tightens the effect considerably ("absence"/"tense," "kill"/"ill"); we should also notice the intense relationship of meaning that prevails between these rhymed words:

> Azure day
> makes my agonized blue window bleaker.
> Crows maunder on the petrified fairway.
> Absence! My heart grows tense
> as though a harpoon were sparring for the kill.
> (This is the house for the "mentally ill.")

Lowell offers slight relief in the next stanza by drawing brief but telling portraits of two other hospital patients. Though the mood is a little more easy, and even humorous at moments, he has already questioned whether his "sense of humor" has any value in the misery of his position. The men portrayed are pitiful examples of human waste: "Stanley, now sunk in his sixties,/once a Harvard all-American fullback," who cares only for his muscular, boyish physique and is "more cut off from words than a seal"; and "Bobbie,"

> Porcellian '29,
> a replica of Louis XVI

without the wig—
redolent and roly-poly as a sperm whale,
as he swashbuckles about in his birthday suit
and horses at chairs.

The athlete and the member of an exclusive Harvard club have "ossified young," and again one observes in Lowell's judgment an off-hand criticism of the society that molded them. In the last stanza the poet returns to himself, though the added knowledge of the futile lives of Stanley and Bobbie has now increased—if that is possible—the seriousness of his plight. Yet a robust and congenial image of Lowell, well-fed and sportily dressed, greets us at the beginning of the stanza. Self-contemplation in the metal shaving mirror, which, like the locked razor, is designed to prevent violence or suicide, deflates his assurance as he imagines the prospects for old age in this hospital. He sees himself among the long-term or permanent inmates, and the poem finishes on a note of quiet frustration:

> Cock of the walk
> I strut in my turtle-necked French sailor's jersey
> before the metal shaving mirrors,
> and see the shaky future grow familiar
> in the pinched, indigenous faces
> of these thoroughbred mental cases,
> twice my age and half my weight.
> We are all old-timers,
> each of us holds a locked razor.

The climate of *Life Studies* is not always so harsh, though it is in general a painful book. Lowell's ironic humor occasionally breaks this spell, and there are instances of tenderness and love, especially in "Home After Three Months Away" and "Man and Wife." *Life Studies* has, over and above the success of many of its poems, the virtue of being a wholly integrated book in which all the parts fit and the prose supports the poetry. It further shows Lowell directing his work away from the elaborate, the baroque and metaphysical, and aiming for a more open statement and form, a language nearer to ordinary speech. The complete disappearance of religious elements and symbolism may be counted an aesthetic loss of sorts, since it removes a center of moral vision from the poetry. Still, as Lowell suggests, religious symbols do not of themselves make a poem religious, and we can justifiably think that sometimes in *Land of Unlikeness* and *Lord Weary's Castle* they obscure a clear apprehension of experience or manufacture a rhetoric of their own. *Life Studies* brings its author firmly to earth, to his individual life, and to a fresh look at the rudiments of poetic style. Since *Life Studies* Lowell has published various poems in magazines (now gathered into the book *For the Union Dead*, 1964) and has, in addition, concentrated on translations and "versions" of foreign poems. In 1961 his translation of Racine's *Phèdre* appeared and also his fascinating *Imitations*, containing renderings of poems by Sappho, Villon, Rilke, Pasternak, Rimbaud, Montale, Baudelaire, and others. As Lowell says in his introduction to the latter book, we find here "one voice running through many personalities, contrasts, repetitions." The last stanza of his version of Rilke's *Die Tauben* ("Pigeons"), a poem placed apart from his other Rilke pieces and at the end of *Imitations*, seems an oblique but appropriate closing commentary by Lowell on the course of his work—from the metaphysical to the humanistic, if we can apply such terms—thus far:

Over non-existence arches the all-being—
thence the ball thrown almost out of bounds
stings the hand with the momentum of its drop—
body and gravity,
miraculously multiplied by its mania to return.

IX

Richard Wilbur

By general agreement Richard Wilbur is one of the most versatile and brilliant American poets to make his debut since World War II. His intelligence, imaginative agility, command of language, and flexibility of technique are awesome and frequently breathtaking. Yet he is not a poet who has put these gifts to the service of some obsessive theme or vision on which the ultimate significance of his work hangs. On the contrary, his inclinations have attracted him toward the tradition of English lyricism which maintains its center in formalism and wit and musical grace. Thus his natural predecessors can be found most easily not only among the Elizabethan, Metaphysical, and Cavalier poets, but also in Emily Dickinson and A. E. Housman. We should not, however, be misled by these affinities into believing that Wilbur lacks his own voice or that his voice is merely a tissue of other voices from the past. He is a very distinctive poet, and though he has undertaken no major stylistic change in his four volumes, there has been a gradual but quite noticeable sharpening of perception and a corresponding modification of manner. These subtle alterations become clearer in his two latest collections, *Things of This World*

(1956) and *Advice to a Prophet* (1961). Throughout his poetry are qualities and characteristics that endow it with a particular identity and may help to account for its appeal.

To begin with, Wilbur is a poet of ceaseless celebrations. As Frederic E. Faverty has said in his essay on Wilbur in *Poets in Progress*, whereas the prevailing mood of much twentieth-century literature has been tragic or negative, this poet, who doesn't try to deny those elements in our experience, still chooses to bring his imagination into contact with other, now somewhat fashionably neglected, aspects of life. The subject, at least the main one, of Wilbur's poetic celebration is the world of *things*. I am certain he would agree in principle with Wallace Stevens' view in "Esthétique du Mal" (without adopting all of Stevens' philosophical ideas) that "The greatest poverty is not to live/In a physical world." The *things* on which Wilbur lavishes his artistic care are not limited to any specific category, no more than are his techniques for treating them poetically. Two poems, one early, one late, will show something of the variety of these *things* that catch his alert interest. The first poem, "Poplar, Sycamore," from *The Beautiful Changes* (1947), is a rich, though brief, descriptive piece on those trees. What we are aware of at once is the wealth of implication his language and rhythm give to the objects of his attention. The poplar seems to gather into its wind-blown motions and its relationships with earth, air, and sky a meaning extracted from the very heart of existence, a meaning of which it is the untranslatable embodiment:

> Poplar, absolute danseuse,
> Wind-wed and faithless to wind, trowelling air
> Tinily everywhere faster than air can fill,
> Here whitely rising, there
> Winding, there
> Feinting to earth with a greener spill,

Never be still, whose pure mobility
Can hold up crowding heaven with a tree.

The sycamore is granted by the poet its own peculiar
importance in the next, and final, stanza. In the closing
lines Wilbur speaks most explicitly about the meaning of
this tree, for we learn suddenly that the theme underlying the observation of poplar and sycamore in all their
sensual grandeur is the activity of imagination. Again
we might note another similarity to Wallace Stevens,
who spent his poetic career exploring the transformation
of physical reality by the faculty of imagination. For
Wilbur the body of the world perceived in its particulars
(here the two trees) stirs the poet/observer's imagination
to take up the possibilities for meditation inherent in
them. What Wilbur is talking about in this stanza applies perhaps first of all to the poet, who goes further
than meditation and creates a poem containing the implications his imagination has discovered—the "more"
than what is seen of the last line. But surely he is not re-
stricting this activity of mind to artists alone; it is a
human potentiality. Here, then, is the sycamore:

Sycamore, trawled by the tilt sun,
Still scrawl your trunk with tattered lights,
    and keep
The spotted toad upon your patchy bark,
Baffle the sight to sleep,
Be such a deep
Rapids of lacing light and dark,
My eye will never know the dry disease
Of thinking things no more than what he sees.

Like Stevens and Roethke, Wilbur singles out the eye
as the most prominent vehicle of imagination. In his
recent *Advice to a Prophet*, the poem "Stop" again exemplifies Wilbur's devotion to *things* in his verse. He

bestows the same loving concern on what is frankly un-
poetic, even beneath ordinary regard or scrutiny, that he
did on the much more promising and conventionally
artistic material of poplar and sycamore trees. In fact,
"Stop" surpasses the merely descriptive; it concludes on
a different plane from the one on which it begins. The
imagination carries it over, through the device of simile,
into mythological suggestiveness, so that the ugly and
the commonplace are redeemed by a hidden radiance:

> In grimy winter dusk
> We slowed for a concrete platform;
> The pillars passed more slowly;
> A paper bag leapt up.
>
> The train banged to a standstill.
> Brake-steam rose and parted.
> Three chipped-at blocks of ice
> Sprawled on a baggage-truck.
>
> Out in that glum, cold air
> The broken ice lay glintless,
> But the truck was painted blue
> On side, wheels, and tongue.
>
> A purple, glowering blue
> Like the phosphorus of Lethe
> Or Queen Persephone's gaze
> In the numb fields of the dark.

Among these dreary objects, under a leaden sky, the
poet's eye is caught by the odd, luminous color of a painted
baggage-truck and an imaginative transformation occurs.
The consequence of this apparently aimless glance is a
new vision of things usually looked at without being seen.

In another poem from the same book entitled "Junk,"
Wilbur, borrowing his form from the Anglo-Saxon, care-

fully examines his "neighbor's ashcan." Its contents are the discarded, broken, or worn-out shabby paraphernalia of our lives; the list starts with a split axe handle:

> The shivered shaft
> > rises from a shellheap
> Of plastic playthings,
> > paper plates,
> And the sheer shards
> > of shattered tumblers
> That were not annealed
> > for the time needful.
> At the same curbside,
> > a cast-off cabinet
> Of wavily-warped
> > unseasoned wood
> Waits to be trundled
> > in the trash man's truck.

Looking on all these abandoned, useless, and cheaply made objects the poet first yields to the natural tendency to be done with them completely, to have them removed from sight. But that very desire arouses its contrary, which is obviously a more genuine feeling, and is more complicated as well:

> Haul them off! Hide them!
> > The heart winces
> For junk and gimcrack
> > for jerrybuilt things
> And the men who make them
> > for a little
> > money . . .

This feeling emerges fully a few lines later when Wilbur finds in these random, cast-off pieces a strange dignity, a self-possession and character which their dereliction only magnifies. From that discovery it is just one step further

in the poem to a consideration of the basic materials of
the "junk" objects in their pure state:

> Yet the things themselves
> > in thoughtless honor
> Have kept composure,
> > like captives who would not
> Talk under torture.
> > Tossed from a tailgate
> Where the dump displays
> > its random dolmens,
> Its black barrows
> > and blazing valleys,
> They shall waste in the weather
> > toward what they
> > were.
>
> The sun shall glory
> > in the glitter of glass-chips,
> Foreseeing the salvage
> > of the prisoned sand,
> And the blistering paint
> > peel off in patches,
> That the good grain
> > be discovered again.

Wilbur's admiration grows as he continues beyond the
kinds of things these objects were, the shapes and uses
men had given them, to a kind of rapt attention to their
elemental properties, by means of which they participate
in the life of the cosmos as a whole. We see in this part
of the poem how Wilbur indicates through his imagery
a cycle of death, disintegration, and renewal for the basic
components of the material universe. Words such as
"dolmens," "barrows," and "valleys" are more than reminiscent of death and burial. Indeed, the dump where
these things finally will be tossed *is* their grave; and there
a process of decomposition sets in which the poet records

above with something exceeding simple accuracy. This
process and what follows it begin to assume a symbolic
design; things decompose, to be sure, but they do so in
order to disclose their purest essence, to return to that
essence in preparation for a new creation. Once more
Wilbur completes his imaginative vision with mythological and legendary allusion:

> Then burnt, bulldozed,
> > they shall all be buried
> To the depth of diamonds
> > in the making dark
> Where halt Hephaestus
> > keeps his hammer
> And Wayland's work
> > is worn away.

If these two poems succeed in illustrating Wilbur's
preoccupation with and reverence for *things*, they may
also begin to acquaint the reader with the spiritual atmosphere of this poet's writing. In an early poem, the
title of which is borrowed from the seventeenth-century
poet and meditational writer Thomas Traherne, " 'A
World without Objects is a Sensible Emptiness,' " Wilbur makes it unmistakably clear that those who seek
spiritual reality cannot properly do so by denying the
physical:

> O connoisseurs of thirst,
> Beasts of my soul who long to learn to drink
> Of pure mirage, those prosperous islands are
> > accurst
> That shimmer on the brink
>
> Of absence; auras, lusters,
> And all shinings need to be shaped and borne.
> Think of those painted saints, capped by the early

masters
With bright, jauntily-worn

Aureate plates, or even
Merry-go-round rings.

And at the poem's conclusion we are admonished "wisely" to "watch" for "the spirit's right/Oasis, light incarnate"; the emphasis, of course, falls on that last word. So it is that while Wilbur often journeys to the region of the spiritual—"Junk" and "Poplar, Sycamore" are good evidence of it—he renders his experience with a profusion of language and imagery that fills out the supposedly remote reaches of the spirit with mass and weight and color.

Though there is little of the ascetic mystic in Wilbur's temperament, he is—at least some of the time—a religious poet. But he is not religious in any strict or doctrinal sense of the word; rather, he is deeply concerned with an experience of life and of the universe as sacramental—as possessing a spiritual worth that shines on surfaces but also hides in recesses. His best critics, Frederic Faverty for one, have brought notice to the considerable number of poems that, in one way or another, have to do with painters or painting, and a few others that have sculpture for their subject. The eye, which we said was the chief instrument of imagination for Wilbur, must be understood as very close in its perceivings to the painter's eye as it attends to the reality it will transmute into a picture. In the poem "Objects," he writes of the artist's responsibility to the things that populate our earthly habitation, and of what must be done for them through the power of imagination that they are incapable of doing for themselves. Their inner nature is released for our observation: "Guard and gild what's common, and forget/Uses and prices and names; have

objects speak." Then Wilbur becomes specific and selects the kind of painter who can excellently represent
his aesthetic point:

> There's classic and there's quaint,
> And then there is that devout intransitive eye
> Of Pieter de Hooch: see feinting from his plot of
>   paint
> The trench of light on boards, the much-mended
>   dry
>
> Courtyard wall of brick,
> And sun submerged in beer, and streaming in
>   glasses,
> The weave of a sleeve, the careful and undulant
>   tile.

The religious aspect of Wilbur's verse is created
through the work of this same "intransitive eye" he
praises in Pieter de Hooch, for that eye concentrates the
poet's amazing sensitiveness to the phenomenal world,
to every fluctuation and nuance in his surroundings, and
to the incredible beauty he sees there. His perceptions
lead him to discern spiritual threads woven into the texture of what his sight finds out, while his impressive
learning, which he carries effortlessly, helps him to articulate his discoveries by metaphor. The poem "October
Maples, Portland" gets started with lyrical description,
introduces a religious theme, and ends in a Christian
legend that illuminates everything that has preceded it:

> The leaves, though little time they have to live,
> Were never so unfallen as today,
> And seem to yield us through a rustled sieve
> The very light from which time fell away.
>
> A showered fire we thought forever lost
> Redeems the air. Where friends in passing meet,

They parley in the tongues of Pentecost.
Gold ranks of temples flank the dazzled street.

It is a light of maples, and will go;
But not before it washes eye and brain
With such a tincture, such a sanguine glow
As cannot fail to leave a lasting stain.

So Mary's laundered mantle (in the tale
Which like all pretty tales, may still be true), ·
Spread on the rosemary-bush, so drenched the pale
Slight blooms in its irradiated hue,
They could not choose but to return in blue.

The natural world in its particular season and through
its lovely brightness of detail is changed in the poet's eye,
and through his deft use of analogy and allusion, into
a sacramental reality: the zones of the spiritual and the
material draw together momentarily in the poem, there
to be experienced again and again. But this instant of
fusion also delineates a boundary for Wilbur's vision;
his poems do not cross it in search of a more direct mystical communion. He always keeps to his insistence in
"Objects" on the necessity of a bond with physical reality.
As Robert Herrick—whom he resembles somewhat in
the ease and perfection with which he writes—employed
fixed forms, and instinctively picked the right tone and
phrase, so Wilbur is essentially a poet of the sensible
world and of its implications. But one should add that he
is not so attracted to the composition of erotic and amatory verse as Herrick was. His sense of the comic and his
ability to produce it in poetry are, however, great—as his
successful translations of Molière's *Misanthrope* and *Tar-
tuffe*, his lyrics for the Lillian Hellman–Leonard Bern-
stein comic-opera version of Voltaire's *Candide*, and some
of his shorter poems amply witness. Wilbur ranges in
these different works from the barbed wit of Molière to

the whimsical feeling of "Epistemology," which consists of just two couplets:

I

Kick at the rock, Sam Johnson, break your bones:
But cloudy, cloudy is the stuff of stones.

II

We milk the cow of the world, and as we do
We whisper in her ear, "You are not true."

Wilbur's talent for the comic takes marvelous form in the elegant bawdiness of "Pangloss's Song: A Comic-Opera Lyric" from *Candide*. Pangloss, wasting away with venereal disease, still contrives to offer a universal hymn of praise to sexual love. These first three stanzas give an adequate impression of the whole piece:

> Dear boy, you will not hear me speak
>   With sorrow or with rancor
> Of what has paled my rosy cheek
>   And blasted it with canker;
> 'Twas Love, great Love, that did the deed
>   Through Nature's gentle laws,
> And how should ill effects proceed
>   From so divine a cause?
>
> Sweet honey comes from bees that sting,
>   As you are well aware;
> To one adept in reasoning,
>   Whatever pains disease may bring
> Are but the tangy seasoning
>   To Love's delicious fare.
>
> Columbus and his men, they say,
>   Conveyed my virus hither
> Whereby my features rot away
>   And vital powers wither;

> Yet had they not traversed the seas
> And come infected back,
> Why think of all the luxuries
> That modern life would lack!

Wilbur has demonstrated skill and beauty in his translations of lyric poetry from the French, Spanish, and Italian, as well as in his versions of Molière. Lyrics by Francis Jammes, Jorge Guillén, Quasimodo, Valéry, Baudelaire, and others, stand firmly in Wilbur's translations as fine poems in English. Each of them seems chosen because of a certain kinship of spirit between the foreign poem and the artistic personality of the translator. In other words, they are poems of a kind Wilbur himself might conceivably have written; in the act of translating he has apparently entered so intimately into an experience of the original that a new poem has been born of it in another language. The watchfulness, the notation of detail, and the final realization of an underlying or symbolic meaning in what is being looked at that we find in his lovely treatment of Guillén's "The Horses" are features of Wilbur's own art:

> Shaggy and heavily natural, they stand
> Immobile under their thick and cumbrous manes,
> Pent in a barbed enclosure which contains,
> By way of compensation, grazing-land.
>
> Nothing disturbs them now. In slow increase
> They fatten like the grass. Doomed to be idle,
> To haul no cart or wagon, wear no bridle,
> They grow into a vegetable peace.
>
> Soul is the issue of so strict a fate.
> They harbor visions in their waking eyes,
> And with their quiet ears participate
> In heaven's pure serenity which lies

So near all things—yet from the beasts concealed.
Serene now, superhuman, they crop their field.

The poems discussed in these pages should warn us
that Richard Wilbur is not the sort of poet from whom
we can abstract a systematic view of life after the fashion
of Yeats, Eliot, or many another modern poet. He is
probably better called an occasional poet of the finest
kind. "What is in a poem is essentially the same as that
which is in one's own life," Goethe says; and this little
dictum applies nicely to Wilbur and his poems, which
so often have their foundation in the chance occasion
of a thought or a visual observation. Take the poem
called "A Hole in the Floor," dedicated to the French
surrealist artist René Magritte, who has painted precise
images of dreams and the subconscious:

> The carpenter's made a hole
> In the parlor floor, and I'm standing
> Staring down into it now
> At four o'clock in the evening,
> As Schliemann stood when his shovel
> Knocked on the crowns of Troy.
>
> A clean-cut sawdust sparkles
> On the grey, shaggy laths,
> And here is a cluster of shavings
> From the time when the floor was laid.
> They are silvery-gold, the color
> Of Hesperian apple-parings.
>
> Kneeling, I look in under
> Where the joists go into hiding.
> A pure street, faintly littered
> With bits and strokes of light,
> Enters the long darkness
> Where its parallels will meet.

> The radiator-pipe
> Rises in middle distance
> Like a shuttered kiosk, standing
> Where the only news is night.
> Here it's not painted green,
> As it is in the visible world.
>
> For God's sake, what am I after?
> Some treasure, or tiny garden?
> Or that untrodden place,
> The house's very soul,
> Where time has stored our footbeats
> And the long skein of our voices?
>
> Not these, but the buried strangeness
> Which nourishes the known:
> That spring from which the floor-lamp
> Drinks now a wilder bloom,
> Inflaming the damask love-seat
> And the whole dangerous room.

Wilbur makes his poem resemble a surrealist painting (but not a surrealist poem): the objects of everyday reality—here, in this case, parts of a house—are transformed almost magically into counters for an unseen psychic world. Things that are perfectly commonplace threaten, under these circumstances, to become something much more mysterious. But, characteristically, Wilbur does not linger in this subterranean place; in the final stanza he comments to his reader on the value of a descent below the surface of the quotidian. His valuation rests on the knowledge that the familiar and visible are enriched by the unknown that lies just under their surface.

Perhaps because of the urbanity and sophistication of his poetic manner, critics have seldom noted the moral element informing a considerable portion of Wilbur's writing. I do not, of course, imply that he is addicted to the platitude or to easy moral generalizations; rather, he tends to handle the poetic events he creates in a way that involves his own deepest instincts and considered judgments. Sometimes judgment inheres in a disarming lightness of touch; sometimes, as in his poem "Advice to a Prophet," it is expanded into a more comprehensive imaginative vision. In that poem—one of Wilbur's best —he advises a prophet how he may convince men of their folly by an appropriate illustration of the type of penalty they can expect to bring upon themselves. This poem may likewise be said to be an occasional one, arising from the hostility and terror of the world's present condition, but the importance of its theme might be felt under any such situation. As we read through the opening stanzas we find the poet enumerating, then discarding, various threats to the continued existence of man on this earth as insufficiently strong to deter him:

> Spare us all word of weapons, their force and
>   range,
> The long numbers that rocket the mind;
> Our slow, unreckoning hearts will be left behind,
> Unable to fear what is too strange.
>
> Nor shall you scare us with talk of the death of
>   the race.
> How should we dream of this place without us?

Alternatively, the poet tells the prophet, "Speak of the world's own change"; and in the stanzas that follow Wilbur proceeds to show us, through a fullness of imagery and metaphor, how the natural world—trees and rivers, birds and beasts—could alienate itself, voluntarily, from man, leaving him alone in a universe that has robbed him of the meanings for himself and his life he had once found reflected there:

Ask us, prophet, how we shall call
Our natures forth when that live tongue is all
Dispelled, that glass obscured or broken

In which we have said the rose of our love and the
        clean
Horse of our courage, in which beheld
The singing locust of the soul unshelled,
And all we mean or wish to mean.

Ask us, ask us whether with the worldless rose
Our hearts shall fail us; come demanding
Whether there shall be lofty or longstanding
When the bronze annals of the oak-tree close.

If, after four volumes, Richard Wilbur has undertaken
no radical overthrow of his earlier manner, has sought
no new and different forms simply for the sake of nov-
elty, we should hardly criticize him for that. From the
outset of his career his art has embodied the highest lyrical qualities, demanded the strictest standards of craftsmanship, and proposed a compassionate and reverential
attitude toward life that has grown into a constant, mature spiritual outlook. One cannot ask for much more.

X

Denise Levertov

American poetry at the present time sustains two extremes, with a wide range of practice in between in which the best—as well as the most truly advanced—writing is usually done. One extreme is represented by the academic poets. The term does not necessarily apply to all poets who happen to teach in universities for their living, but denotes those writers whose materials are often selected from the history of literature and culture, and whose methods are dictated by the critical theories of what poetry ought to be. At the opposite extreme, the Hip writers mistake the exhibition of hysteria and the release of invective, unhindered by the requirements of craft, for poetry. Whitman and Rimbaud, the "true gods" the Hip writers claim for their masters, had both the genius and the strength to navigate the rapids of emotion and vision in which these self-styled successors capsize and drown.

At the same moment—around 1957—that such figures as Ginsberg and Kerouac began to make news, a number of other, previously little-known, poets also published their own books and caused a less sensational but more worthy stir. Some of them may even have been loosely associated in the minds of their audience with the Hip writers next to whom they were occasionally printed; but there is little resemblance except in their mutual rejection of the ruling literary and critical modes. And these poets differ greatly among one another as well. All of them, however—and I include here poets such as Robert Creeley, Paul Carroll, Frank O'Hara, John Ashbery, Barbara Guest, Gary Snyder, David Ignatow, Brother Antoninus, Galway Kinnell, and John Logan, in addition to Denise Levertov—aim at an expression of the most personal kind of experience, an authentic statement about themselves, what they see and know, suffer and love; their responses to the things, relationships, and heightened instants of their lives. The tendencies of these poets lead them to the repudiation of Eliot's belief in an "objective correlative" that screens the artist from his work and maintains the privacy of his life as an individual. The idea of masks that explains so much modern poetry of the post-Symbolist generation has no value for these younger poets, who really walk naked, as Yeats said poets should.

We have considered in a previous chapter how the poetry of Robert Lowell moves into this same area of the highly personal or confessional, though he comes from a very different corner of the literary map than does Denise Levertov or Robert Creeley or David Ignatow. The latter have steeped themselves for a long time in that tradition of modern writing whose pioneers are William Carlos Williams, Ezra Pound, and H. D.

Among her fellow-poets in this tradition, Denise Levertov stands out as one whose art, fresh and compelling, convinces us of her genuine rapport with the reality she presents as its core. Her poetry is frequently a tour through the familiar and the mundane until their unfamiliarity and otherworldliness suddenly strike us. Her imaginative gaze feasts on the small objects we usually treat as insignificant appendages to our lives, or pauses with affectionate interest on the seemingly trivial activities in which we spend so much of those lives. Thus she engages very naturally in a persistent investigation of the events of her own life—inner and outer—in the language of her own time and place, and completes that investigation in the forms emerging from what she discovers as it is translated into words. Miss Levertov shares the spirit of Martin Buber, for she always says "thou" to the persons, occasions, and objects she encounters; that is her imagination's essential humanizing gesture toward every aspect of existence.

As I have already indicated, Miss Levertov, along with a variety of other poets, departs sharply from the poetic and critical line passing down through Yeats, Eliot, Auden, and the critics who have developed aesthetic views from their initiative. In the introduction to his anthology *Contemporary American Poetry*, Donald Hall offers a good summary description of qualities emphasized by the poets working in the opposing tradition, with its foundation in the example of William Carlos Williams. "This poetry," Hall tells us, "is no mere restriction of one's vocabulary. It wants to use the language with the intimacy acquired in unrehearsed unliterary speech. But it has other characteristics which are not linguistic. It is a poetry of experiences more than of ideas. The experience is presented often without comment, and the words of the description must supply the emotion which the experience generates, without generalization or summary."

In allying herself with this movement, Miss Levertov had to grapple with prevailing literary modes and, finally, to discard them. A struggle of this sort, the purpose of which is to open a way for poetic development, normally makes or breaks a writer—that is, if he or she dares to undertake it, as many do not—and it is a real sign of Miss Levertov's abilities that she has returned victorious. But the effort to win a voice of one's own amounts to nothing or becomes artificial unless it has been prompted by the conditions of human experience itself, by all that is cast into the poet's field of vision in the course of living. Poetry, if it will earn its name, must never begin with experience at second hand, but with a steady eye on what surrounds us everywhere. As the French philosopher Jacques Maritain says in his *Art and Scholasticism,* "Our art does not derive from itself alone what it imparts to things; it spreads over them a secret which it first discovered in them, in their invisible substance or in their endless exchanges and correspondences." Miss Levertov has learned this lesson well, and it is identical to the one her art teaches us. The conclusion of her "Note on the Work of the Imagination" (*New Directions 17,* edited by James Laughlin) adds to the quotation from Maritain a consideration of this spiritual faculty which makes the poetic object possible; she writes, "What joy to be reminded . . . that the Imagination does not arise from the environment but has the power to create it!"

Some poets make their published poems the battleground for style and individuality, and the reader can witness the spectacle, and its success or failure. In Denise Levertov there is an unseen conflict which occurred somewhere in the eleven-year span between her first book, *The Double Image* (1946), published in England before she came to the United States, and her next, *Here and Now* (1957), issued by Lawrence Ferlinghetti's City Lights Bookshop in San Francisco. Kenneth Rexroth, who anthologized her work some years ago in his *New British Poets,* placed her then as one of the most promising neo-romantics of the war period; but his later statements about her writing, collected in *Assays* (1961), indicate that he believes—as I do—Miss Levertov's full powers as a poet began to unleash themselves only after she had been in America awhile and, as Rexroth says, had come "to talk like a mildly internationalized young

woman living in New York but alive to all the life of
speech in the country."

The poems included in *The Double Image* give evidence of a true poetic gift in their author, though they
are not marked with those characteristics of thought and
rhythm and speech that would insure them as her handi-
work, and hers alone. I don't mean that the poems are
imitations; on the other hand, they seem to partake of
a general mood in English poetry of the time, owing, no
doubt, to the war. Here is world-weariness, disenchant-
ment, a flirtatiousness with death and the twilight regions of the spirit. Somehow a vein of uncertainty runs
through these pieces, as if the poet almost suspected herself in what she was doing. I am sure, however, that I
could never gain such an impression if Miss Levertov had
published only that single volume or if she had continued in her initial style. She served her poetic apprenticeship in works suffused with vague emotion, filled with
whispers of mortality and unrest, the damp vegetation
of England, and murmurs of perishable love. I will quote
just a few lines from one of these early poems, "Five
Aspects of Fear," before approaching her more central
productions:

> In fear of floods, long quenched, waves fallen,
> shattered mirrors darken with old cries;
> where no shot sounds the frightened birds go flying
> over heights of autumn soft as honey:
> each country left is full of our own ghosts
> in fear of floods quenched, waves fallen.
> Rags of childhood flutter in the woods
> and each deserted post has sentinels;
> bright eyes in wells watch for the sun's assassin:
> the regions bereft of our desires are haunted,
> rags of childhood flutter in the woods.

Something of the Georgians lingers on in this passage
with its rural withdrawal from contemporary affairs, but

the strongest and most obvious pull is toward Surrealism,
which had crossed the channel in the 1930s and was still
a strong influence during the war. Miss Levertov tries,
by means of dreamlike associations and indefiniteness of
imagery, to articulate as nearly as possible the purity of
her emotions, unsoiled by the concrete or the particular.
That vagueness is far removed from what we have come
to know as the essential poet in her, the poet whose
sleeves are rolled and who wrestles up to her elbows in the
dust of a common world. In this poem the effects are at-
mospheric; the words, I believe, are supposed to bear a
cumulative weight of feeling *apart* from any denotation.
How different from the present Denise Levertov, who
senses her materials as a Giacometti or a David Hare
senses the materials of his sculpture. Her "Pleasures," as
she calls them in the title of a later poem, are now quite
altered:

> I like to find
> what's not found
> at once, but lies
>
> within something of another nature,
> in repose, distinct.
> Gull feathers of glass, hidden
>
> in white pulp: the bones of a squid
> which I pull out and lay
> blade by blade on the draining board—
>
> > tapered as if for swiftness, to pierce
> > the heart, but fragile, substance
> > belying design. Or a fruit, *mamey,*
>
> cased in rough brown peel, the flesh
> rose-amber, and the seed:
> the seed a stone of wood, carved and

      polished, walnut-colored, formed
      like a brazilnut, but large,
      large enough to fill
      the hungry palm of a hand.

   The reader will not be wrong, I think, if he sees in this poem, behind its fascination with the beauty of small objects and concealed things, an allegorical statement of the poet's own concern with material reality. In forcing tangible things to disclose their truths and felicities, she urges human reality to yield some of its secrets—and its covert analogies and predilections too.

   The change that takes place between her first and second books—in a decade that saw Miss Levertov leave England, travel in Europe, meet the American novelist Mitchell Goodman, marry him, and settle in this country—is remarkable and must have demanded no less than a complete renovation of her poetic values. But this revolution of the heart, the head, the senses, how worthwhile it all was! She was compelled to start from scratch, and that meant for Miss Levertov a confrontation of the happenings of her life. What she so shrewdly observed was that the ordinary is extraordinarily unusual:

      What a sweet smell rises
      when you lay the dust—
      bucket after bucket of water thrown
      on the yellow grass.
                     The water
    flashes
    each time you
    make it leap—
                 arching its glittering back.
   The sound of
             more water
    pouring into the pail
    almost quenches my thirst.

> Surely when flowers
> grow here, they'll not
> smell sweeter than this
>   wet ground, suddenly black.

Of course, as Kenneth Rexroth further noted, Miss Levertov came under novel influences in America that were quite unlike any English ones. He names as a chief influence the poet we have already mentioned, the writer whose lessons she must have learned well, though without sacrificing her own intentions and capacities. That poet is the late William Carlos Williams. It is likely that she also learned from Rexroth's own poetry and from the Imagists; in her moving tribute to H. D. entitled "Summer 1961," she records some of her debts to Williams, Pound, and H. D.:

> They have told us
> the road leads to the sea,
> and given
>
> the language into our hands.

Perhaps if we look at a brief but fairly representative poem by Williams to remind ourselves of certain qualities in his work we will be able to determine, by comparison with Miss Levertov's "Laying the Dust" above, some of their similarities. Williams' poem is called "Between Walls":

> the back wings
> of the
>
> hospital where
> nothing
>
> will grow lie
> cinders

in which shine
the broken

pieces of a green
bottle

Clearly, this poem has little relation to the kind of
poetry in the ascendency during the first half of the
twentieth century; the poetry of the French Symbolists
has had no bearing on what we read in these lines. Again,
if we try to apply the sort of exegesis to Williams' poetry
—or to Miss Levertov's, for that matter—that is used on
Eliot's or Rilke's or Valéry's, we shall miss the point and
look foolish. Ingenious explication is beside the point here
and will bury the meaning of both poems; we should do
better to contemplate them as we would a painting. Williams' attraction to the *disjecta membra* of the physical
world, particularly of the modern urban setting, set a
firm precedent for Miss Levertov's own poetic venture.
We should not forget, either, Williams' insistence that
the moral responsibility of the American poet lies in
using his native tongue "to represent what his mind per-
ceives directly about him," because this endeavor is, to
a degree, Miss Levertov's. Yet there is also a gradual inward turning in her latest poetry and an increasing preoccupation with parable, dream, and interior illumination that are foreign to Williams' imagination.

Williams was for years a champion of younger writers
in the United States and, further, was a stalwart foe of
the post-Symbolist literature of Yeats and Eliot, as well
as an opponent of what he thought was an outworn tradition of English verse forms and meters. It is hardly by
accident, then, that young poets, in search of a way past
the official poetic idiom, looked to Williams' writings
and his viewpoint for guidance. The rejection of conventional for organic form; the repudiation of established

metrical patterns in favor of what Williams called "the variable foot"; the return to the spoken language, the *American* spoken language—these are some of the most prominent results of the senior poet's influence. These younger poets likewise avoid in general the habit of making their work a repository of intellectual history, learning, and fragments of the European cultural heritage. I should like to call the poetry of Miss Levertov, and that of a number of her contemporaries, "poetry of the immediate."

My term requires some explanation. I do not mean by "the immediate" an art without craftsmanship, an art that fixes on the disorder of sheer impulse or emotional notation. Miss Levertov has never allowed her poetry to become even slightly vulnerable to that kind of charge—a glance at any one of her poems will prove it. Moreover, we need only cite the comment she supplies for Donald Allen's anthology *The New American Poetry 1945-1960*, where there is no mistaking her distaste for sloppy composition: "I long for poems," she writes, "of an inner harmony in utter contrast to the chaos in which they exist." Poetry must not be a shapeless replica of external things but an organically formed transfiguration of them in which the transfiguration, rather than poetic convention, dictates the form. What I call "the immediate," then, signifies the complex of relationships existing between the poet and the elements that are close at hand in her personal experience. The things, the happenings, the thoughts and dreams that are subjective events in themselves—everything that falls within the circumference of the poet's life as an individual—become the matter of poetry. The author's private circumstance is explored, its potentialities drawn out; but however far her speculations lead her, Miss Levertov never oversteps that circumference. Instead, she creates from within herself an attitude with which to face her environment, as in her poem "Something to Wear":

To sit and sit like the cat
and think my thoughts through—
that might be a deep pleasure:

to learn what news
persistence might discover,
and like a woman knitting

make something from the
skein unwinding, unwinding,
something I could wear

or something you could wear
when at length I rose to meet you
outside the quiet sitting-room

(the room of thinking and knitting
the room of cats and women)
among the clamor of

cars and people,
the stars drumming and poems
leaping from shattered windows.

This poem grows around the mind's self-reflective activity. While poems about poetry, the act of composition, or the mind contemplating its own powers and
processes are common in the literary history of the past
170 years—Mallarmé and Wallace Stevens, for example,
expended much of their artistic energy on these themes
—Denise Levertov treats such matters in a more personal, autobiographical way than most previous poets
have done. Mallarmé, in his famous sonnet, "La vierge,
le vivace et le bel aujourd'hui," depicts the poet's failure
of imagination through the remote but lovely symbolic
image of a swan trapped in ice and earthbound:

Un cygne d'autrefois se souvient que c'est lui
Magnifique mais qui sans espoir se délivre
Pour n'avoir pas chanté le région où vivre
Quand du stérile hiver a resplendi l'ennui.

(A swan of former times remembers it is he
Magnificent but who without hope gives himself up
For not having sung of the region where he should
    have been
When the boredom of sterile winter was
    resplendent.)

            (Translation by Wallace Fowlie,
            from *Mallarmé*, 1953.)

But however acutely the poet has felt the anguish of impotence in his art, he has removed those feelings from the sphere of his own life and incorporated them into the symbolic universe of his poetry. Stevens is less divided; indeed, his notebooks indicate that he wished to have his theory of the imagination become a cosmic view that could be shared by all men. Nonetheless, Stevens' poetry is generally impersonal and almost totally divorced from the important details of his existence as a man. Miss Levertov does not recognize such separations and refuses to hide her life from her imagination. Yet she may have learned from Stevens—as well as from her own thoughts or from other poets' work—that poetry can be involved in the mind's activity as an individual goes about his daily business of registering and interpreting and responding to surrounding reality. The poem "Something to Wear" describes in part the preparations the mind or self makes to encounter this reality ("the clamor of/cars and people . . .") and to elicit from it the substance of art and beauty ("the stars drumming and poems/leaping from shattered windows"). The contemplating self of the poem's beginning does not keep

to solitude but, as in "Matins," vii, goes out to meet the
world and come upon the stuff of poetry there:

> Marvelous Truth, confront us
> at every turn,
> in every guise, iron ball,
> egg, dark horse, shadow,
> cloud
> of breath on the air,
>
> dwell
> in our crowded hearts
> our steaming bathrooms, kitchens full of
> things to be done, the
> ordinary streets.
>
> Thrust close your smile
> that we know you, terrible joy.

Thus for Denise Levertov, as for certain other poets,
it is proper, even imperative, for the literary enterprise
to concentrate on assigning judgment and value, on finding the marvelous, within the particular range of personal observation and knowledge. If such writing is crit-
icized for a lack of ambitious scope, one might reply
that it compensates by a penetrating and scrupulous
honesty, by a fundamental human resonance that is
anything but restricted, and by a fidelity to the experience of contemporary life. Younger writers today, of
almost every allegiance or group, have withdrawn their
efforts from the elaboration of symbolic systems and
mythologies; the Cantos, The Waste Land, The Duino
Elegies, although they are still widely admired, apparently are looked upon as distant accomplishments. Now
the poet believes he must use his art to define the space
he inhabits as a person—if I may be permitted the figure
—the space in which he exists, chooses and asserts value,
loves and hates and dies. And so for Miss Levertov the

poem is an instrument of personal measure, of tests and balances, estimating and preserving the valuable in the teeth of a public actuality that day by day magnifies its impersonality, falsity, and unreality. A poem such as "The Instant" rises out of personal experience and the depth of genuine emotion and significance attached to it by the author. As Miss Levertov's own testament the poem cannot be refuted or denied, for it stands well inside the space her poetic imagination circumscribes about her life as she lives it. Here is the complete poem, taken from her third book *Overland to the Islands* (1958); to cut it would be to destroy the form of an experience as she has realized it:

"We'll go out before breakfast, and get
some mushrooms," says my mother.

Early, early: the sun
risen, but hidden in mist

the square house left behind
sleeping, filled with sleepers;

up the dewy hill, quietly with baskets.
Mushrooms firm, cold;
      tussocks of dark grass, gleam of webs,
turf soft and cropped. Quiet and early. And no
      valley

no hills: clouds about our knees, tendrils
of cloud in our hair. Wet scrags
of wool caught in barbed wire, gorse
looming, without scent.
                      Then ah! suddenly

the lifting of it, the mist rolls
      quickly away, and far, far—

> "Look!" she grips me, "It is
>   Eryri!
>   It's Snowdon, fifty
> miles away!"—the voice
> a wave rising to Eryri,
> falling.
>
>
>   Snowdon, home
> of eagles, resting-place of
> Merlin, core of Wales.
>
>
>   Light
> graces the mountainhead
> for a lifetime's look, before the mist
>   draws in again.

This poem is both an abbreviated narrative, dramatic in character (in this it resembles many poems by Robert Creeley, Paul Carroll, and others), and a spiritual adventure of a nearly ineffable sort. Within the tradition of post-Symbolist literature such a private illumination as the poet has here would be objectified into the order of a larger metaphorical universe—which is not to say that its value would be sacrificed, but that the value would be transmuted. But in the present poem the experience remains unchanged, is viewed in its own terms. Miss Levertov molds the event into art without abandoning the quality of direct utterance or leaving the domain of her life. The instant to which the poem's title refers is the moment of enlightenment that occurs when mist and clouds part to expose the far-off mountain peak shining in the early light of day and richly endowed with legendary meaning. Still, the poem retains its status as a poem of fact, so to speak, emerging from ordinary circumstances and immediate life, and returning there. We are acquainted with this kind of illumination in Blake or Rilke, though for them it confirms the basis of a whole mythological scheme: the world of things ablaze with the eternal Being they mirror. But to find any metaphysical revelation in Miss Levertov's art we must enter the precincts of the poet's own existence, for she justifies her art through that existence, as well as her existence through her artistic perception.

Miss Levertov's primary intention as a poet has not been the statement of visionary experiences but rather the dogged probing of all the routine business of life in search of what she calls "the authentic" in its rhythms and its details. Her marriage may be a subject for investigation:

> I want to speak to you.
> To whom else should I speak?
> It is you who make
> a world to speak of.
> In your warmth the
> fruits ripen—all the
> apples and pears that grow
> on the south wall of my
> head. If you listen
> it rains for them, then
> they drink. If you
> speak in response
> the seeds
> jump into the ground.
> Speak or be silent: your silence
> will speak to me.
> ("The Marriage, II")

or the city's winter streets and the snatches of conversation overheard there:

> As the stores close, a winter light
>   opens air to iris blue,
>   glint of frost through the smoke,
>   grains of mica, salt of the sidewalk.

As the buildings closed, released autonomous
    feet pattern the streets
    in hurry and stroll; balloon heads
    drift and dive above them; the bodies
    aren't really there.

As the lights brighten, as the sky darkens,
    a woman with crooked heels says to another
        woman
    while they step along at a fair pace,

    *"You know, I'm telling you, what I love best
    is life. I love life! Even if I ever get
    to be old and wheezy—or limp! You know?*

    Limping along?—I'd still . . ." Out of hearing.

To the multiple disordered tones
    of gears changing, a dance
    to the compass points, out, a four-way river.

Prospect of sky
    wedged into avenues, left at the ends of streets,
    west sky, east sky: more life tonight! A range
    of open time at winter's outskirts.
                    ("February Evening in New York")

This delighted involvement with what most of us continually neglect as trivia or noise, and the ability to carry
out, as Marianne Moore and William Carlos Williams
do, poetic conquests in the categories of the prosaic, are
so natural to Miss Levertov's temperament that she seems
scarcely to think of them. She is totally alive to each fluctuation, each breath and vibration of the atmosphere
through which she moves with watchful ease. Poetry
speaks to her with the innocent tongues of children:

Martha, 5, scrawling a drawing, murmurs
"These are two angels. These are two bombs. They
are in the sunshine. Magic
is dropping from the angels' wings."

Nik, at 4, called
          over the stubblefield, "Look
the flowers are dancing underneath the
tree, and the tree
          is looking down with all its apple-eyes."

Without hesitation or debate, words
used and at once forgotten.

("The Lesson")

Even though I find it hard to picture Miss Levertov as
an aesthetic theorist musing abstractly upon the rightful
function of poetry in a hyper-industrialized society, I am
sure that in practice poetry is for her an integral part of
the acts, thoughts, and gestures of living. In many of her
poems we cross into a world very like our own, with the
same ornaments and refuse, commonplaces and strokes
of grace, but it is also a world made splendid and different by this poet's wise and clear apprehension of it, her
abundant imagination. Poems do more than leap from
windows; they appear in the humblest, most mundane
things, such as this image, seized from a minute's glance
out of the poet's kitchen window over the city at sunset:

On the kitchen wall a flash
of shadow:
                    swift pilgrimage
of pigeons, a spiral
celebration of air, of sky-deserts.
And on tenement windows
a blaze
          of lustred watermelon:

    stain of the sun
    westering somewhere back of Hoboken.
                    ("The World Outside," I)

The quotidian reality we ignore or try to escape, Denise
Levertov revels in, carves and hammers into lyric poems
of precise beauty. As celebrations and rituals lifted from
the midst of contemporary life in its actual concreteness,
her poems are unsurpassed; they open to us aspects of
object and situation that but for them we should never
have known. And that is no mean achievement for any
poet, though it is not the only one Miss Levertov can
boast. Another side of her work has slowly asserted itself
in two later books, *With Eyes at the Back of Our Heads*
(1959) and *The Jacob's Ladder* (1961). I have already
alluded to this visionary disposition in discussing "The
Instant," but the subsequent pieces rely much more on
dream, mystical imagery, and meditation than they do
on external conditions that are suddenly transfigured.
Some of these poems reflect on the sources of art and
imagination and are developments in the line of "Something to Wear," though they find their materials in a
deeper layer of consciousness. "The Goddess," "The
Well," and "The Illustration," from *The Jacob's Ladder*,
are excellent representatives of this category. Other poems
press forward on a spiritual journey whose purpose is to
uncover the nature of self and its destiny. Miss Levertov's
father was a Russian Jew who later became an Anglican
clergyman; something of this combination, plus her reading in Biblical, Hasidic, and other mystical writings, undoubtedly has had a decisive influence on these poems.

An example of her meditational poetry is the title poem
"With Eyes at the Back of Our Heads"; here Miss Levertov brings to focus two planes of reality that seem to be
distant but somehow border one another. The problem
is how to get from the first into the second, and the poet
addresses herself to it:

With eyes at the back of our heads
we see a mountain
not obstructed with woods but laced
here and there with feathery groves.

The doors before us in a façade
that perhaps has no house in back of it
are too narrow, and one is set too high
with no doorsill. The architect sees

the imperfect proposition and
turns eagerly to the knitter.
Set it to rights!
The knitter begins to knit.

For we want
to enter the house, if there is a house,
to pass through the doors at least
into whatever lies beyond them,

we want to enter the arms
of the knitted garment. As one
is re-formed, so the other,
in proportion.

When the doors widen
when the sleeves admit us
the way to the mountain will clear,
the mountain we see with
eyes at the back of our heads, mountain

green, mountain
cut of limestone, echoing
with hidden rivers, mountain
of short grass and subtle shadows.

Miss Levertov gives us here a parable of the inner life,
a metaphorical presentation of spiritual pilgrimage in the

individual. The heart of the poem appears paradoxical because the mountain, which is an image of paradisaical proportions, a depiction of the Great Good Place, is seen only within, by intuition (the "eyes at the back of our heads"), while the obstacles to be overcome and those to which we have to accommodate ourselves lie before us. Yet, as in Heraclitus and Eliot's *Four Quartets*, the way forward and the way back are one and the same. Thus movement ahead, with the alterations of the self it requires, will be completed in a reconciliation of the inner image of a desired goal with a personal condition of life. Perhaps what we are being told is, "The Kingdom of God is within you." In this, as in her other remarkable poems, Miss Levertov subtly points the way to see with our whole sight.

XI

James Wright

With the publication of his first collection of poems in 1957 it was already clear that James Wright would establish himself as a poet of independence who pursued his artistic goals without regard for the changeable market of literary fashions. From the start of his career to the present time he has dedicated himself single-mindedly to the demands of his art. This independence in Wright's early poetry made him stand out noticeably during a period that produced a plethora of slick and elegant verse sadly lacking in human substance. In the years following it has been encouraging to see the emergence of a resolute poet who has, all along, taken a harder and lonelier course than he might have done. The consequence is impressive: a body of poetry that has grown and matured with its author, increasing in depth and range, expanding in its means of execution.

In *The Green Wall*, chosen by W. H. Auden as an award-winning volume for the Yale Series of Younger Poets, Wright announced that he had "tried very hard to write in the mode of Robert Frost and Edwin Arlington Robinson," and that he "wanted to make the poems say something humanly important instead of just showing off with language." In that initial book, and in his second one, *Saint Judas* (1959), the poet sets himself to this task through poems that are meditations on his own experience, observations of other lives, dramatic situations; his speech is direct, his sympathy and judgment are undisguised. The world called up by his imagination in poetry is unmistakably the one we know, in which people are born, endure pain, discover love, encounter success or defeat in their efforts, and go down to death. It is not a symbolic world or a self-contained poetic cosmos, but a reality composed of men and women, of animals and birds, of stones and trees, and is usually located in the American Midwest, in Ohio and Minnesota where Wright has spent so much time. As a poet he is always able to bring us into contact with the physical details of this reality that is so familiar to him and yet distinct and independent too:

> The stone turns over slowly,
> Under the side one sees
> The pale flint covered wholly
> With whorls and prints of leaf.
> After the moss rubs off
> It gleams beneath the trees,
> Till all the birds lie down.
> Hand, you have held that stone.
> ("A Fit Against the Country")

A number of poems touch on persons or events and are conceived in the same terms of intimate acquaintance and objective existence. Though he looks closely at experience, Wright never tries to maneuver it to his own ends. Frequently, he pauses to study the most ordinary things, which his imagination lifts at last from the limbo of the routine and unworthy in an attempt to search out the meanings lying dormant in them. Each thing has its shadow or hidden life disclosed by the poet.

In the poem "A Girl in the Window," for example,

we learn how Wright can take a commonplace occurrence —his casual view, as he sits outside in the evening, of a girl's attractive silhouette in a lighted window—and from it obtain gentle nuances of feeling, in this case the warm but not lustful affection of flesh for flesh. It is also worth remarking how this literal shadow of a girl exemplifies in a poem the shadow of implication I mentioned metaphorically above. "A Girl in a Window" is, in a certain sense, really about the significance of what would ordinarily seem rather insignificant.

> Now she will lean away to fold
> The window blind and curtain back,
> The yellow arms, the hips of gold,
> The supple outline fading black,
> Bosom availing nothing now,
> And rounded shadow of long thighs.
> How can she care for us, allow
> The shade to blind imagined eyes?
>
> Behind us, where we sit by trees,
> Blundering autos lurch and swerve
> On gravel, crawling on their knees
> Around the unfamiliar curve;
> Further behind, a passing train
> Ignores our lost identity;
> So, reassured, we turn again
> To see her vanish under sky.
>
> Soon we must leave her scene to-night,
> To stars, or the indiscriminate
> Pale accidents of lantern light,
> A watchman walking by too late.
> Let us return her now, my friends,
> Her love, her body to the grave
> Fancy of dreams where love depends.
> She gave, and did not know she gave.

The collective "we" makes of Wright the self-appointed speaker for what are probably other men, anonymous figures who also enjoy the evening air and in their fancy take this girl for their own. Her appearance at the window inspires these lonely watchers to join their lives with hers briefly in imagination.

The tone of Wright's early poetry is conversational and quiet, which helps in preserving the atmosphere of familiarity already noted; but there are poems—primarily those treating what Auden calls in his introduction to *The Green Wall* "social outsiders"—in which an intensification of vision, prophetic of more recent work, occurs. Such poems look toward the frank self-exposure of *Saint Judas*. In the figures of those whose actions have transgressed the conventions of the community, and who, as a result, are converted into scapegoats of society, the poet can discover no guilt greater than the culpability that hides itself behind the masks of their respectable persecutors. "Sappho," a monologue spoken by a lesbian who has carried on an affair with a married woman and has now to suffer the social and moral disapproval of her fellow citizens, concludes with an acceptance of pain, of the body's demands that purges the speaker and elevates her to a position of spiritual dignity far surpassing the one her accusers occupy:

> For I know that I am asked to hate myself
> For their sweet sake
> Who sow the world with child.
> I am given to burn on the dark fire they make
> With their sly voices.
> But I have burned already down to the bone.
> There is a fire that burns beyond the names
> Of sludge and filth of which the world is made.
> Agony sears the dark flesh of the body,
> And lifts me higher than the smoke, to rise
> Above the earth, above the sacrifice;

Until my soul flares outward like a blue
Blossom of gas fire dancing in mid-air:
Free of the body's work of twisted iron.

In another poem, "To a Fugitive," Wright identifies himself with the desperate grasping for freedom and life of an escaped convict. He dreams of the escape, its violence, and a nightmare of pursuit by dogs and police. The final lines direct the fleeing criminal past every barrier and into a transcendental realm of absolute liberty: "Strip, run for it, break the last law, unfold,/Dart down the alley, race between the stars." With other modern poets as dissimilar as E. E. Cummings and Stanley Kunitz, Wright takes the side of the alienated individual, the hunted and persecuted, and opposes the impersonal majority or the monolithic state.

Other poems approach alternate extremities of human experience. Death, to which Wright turns frequently in all of his books, is considered variously through elegies and meditations, and also by means of vision or dream. His religious attitudes cannot be fully determined from such poems, though they are rather obviously heterodox and private. While we sometimes come upon allusions to Christ, to resurrection, and to other religious phenomena in Wright's poetry, a consistent relationship is maintained between the dying or the dead, both human and animal, and the earth whereon they passed their lives. Even the poem "Come Forth," which presents Lazarus' awakening from the sleep of death, unquestionably stresses the ritual reassembling of his body in a celebration of human, earthly existence rather than Christ's miraculous deed. To be sure, a miracle is performed, but the exclamatory closing line focuses on the desirable world to which the dead man has been restored: "O blessed fire, O harsh and loving air."

At times Wright lets the imagination confer its own speculative fate upon the dead, but in these cases the view of things underlying the mental reflections is fundamentally one of stoical resignation. The fine "On the Skeleton of a Hound" is a poem of this sort. Here the poet, walking by moonlight, accidentally comes across the skeleton of his old dog and sees that the remains have not been disturbed but have kept an arrangement suggesting orderly repose. The earth, we are told, "nurses him now," sending its life branching through and around these bones:

> Flies would love to leap
> Between his eyes and hum away the space
> Between his ears, the hollow where a hare
> Could hide; another jealous dog would tumble
> The bones apart, angry, the shining crumble
> Of a great body gleaming in the air;
> Quivering pigeons foul his broken face.

The poet then muses on what a group of primitive believers would do with the skeleton. He imagines them practicing magic in the vain endeavor to revive life:

> I can imagine men who search the earth
> For handy resurrections, overturn
> The body of a beetle in its grave;
> Whispering men digging for gods might delve
> A pocket for these bones, then slowly burn
> Twigs in the leaves, pray for another birth.

Having entertained the contrary images of dissolution and rebirth, Wright dismisses both of them and turns away from this "ruin of summer, collapse of fur and bone."

In the remainder of the poem the author seeks resolution in the subjective area of his individual consciousness, where memory and imagination can write their own finish to the dog's story. So the memory of a life is forged into private legend in the poet's mind, finally becoming fixed in the more permanent form of his art:

For once a white hare huddled up the grass,
The sparrows flocked away to see the race.
I stood on darkness, clinging to a stone,
I saw the two leaping alive on ice,
On earth, on leaf, humus and withered vine:
The rabbit splendid in a shroud of shade,
The dog carved on the sunlight, on the air,
Fierce and magnificent his rippled hair,
The cockleburs shaking around his head.
Then, suddenly, the hare leaped beyond pain
Out of the open meadow, and the hound
Followed the voiceless dancer to the moon,
To dark, to death, to other meadows where
Singing young women dance around a fire,
Where love reveres the living.

The closing image of the circle of dancing women (a similar image occurs in a much later poem, "A Message Hidden in an Empty Wine Bottle . . .") hints at a kind of symbolic eternity, a perpetual ring that is the world of the dead but is still plainly linked to life and the physical universe. More than a meditation on death, this poem illustrates the technique of making the personally meaningful, through the power of imagination, into something bearing a more general significance. The latest of Wright's poetry is in some ways an extension of the process in this piece, but radical changes in style intervene. Scattering the bones of the hound to earth in the last few lines, the poet accompanies his actions with a prophecy, one quite in keeping with his vision of the attachment of the dead for the living in the preceding stanza:

Strewn to the woods, now may that spirit sleep
That flamed over the ground a year ago.
I know the mole will heave a shinbone over,
The earthworm snuggle for a nap on paws,
The honest bees build honey in the head;
The earth knows how to handle the great dead

Who lived the body out, and broke its laws,
Knocked down a fence, tore up a field of clover.

Saint Judas continues most of the interests of Wright's
first book, but a more penetrating insight into the poet's
own person is apparent in many of these poems. The in-
jurious and tragic aspects of existence are examined
freely, and the quality of Wright's poetic speech becomes
even more direct and terse as he attempts relentlessly to
locate and state the human truths that matter to him.
"The Morality of Poetry," a dramatic monologue in
which the poet starts out to formulate a rather strict
aesthetic and ends with a different poetic outlook, is one
of the most arresting pieces in the collection. At the beginning the poet walks by the sea—just as Wallace
Stevens does in his famous monologue on the activity of
poetry, "The Idea of Order at Key West"—thinking over
some words of Whitman on the relation between art and
reality ("Would you the undulation of one wave, its
trick to me transfer . . ."), and at the same time watching in the scene before him the kind of brute material
facts from which his literary predecessor had wished to
wrest artistic secrets:

> I stood above the sown and generous sea
> Late in the day, to muse about your words:
> Your human images come to pray for hands
> To wipe your vision clear, your human voice
> Flinging the poem forward into sound.
> Below me, roaring elegies to birds,
> Intricate, cold, the waters crawled the sands,
> Heaving and groaning, casting up a tree,
> A shell, a can to clamber over the ground:
> Slow celebration, cluttering ripple on wave.

At the start of the second stanza the poet enumerates
the profusion of things in the natural surroundings he
gazes upon. The "sheer outrage" of the sea makes it ap-

pear to be "hammering itself to death," while "hundreds of gulls" descend into the waves but without any particular sense for the writer who views them carefully ("Counting those images, I meant to say/ A hundred gulls decline to nothingness . . ."). This absence of discernible meaning in seemingly random motion and energy, and also in an undifferentiated mass of creatures, proves to be the turning point in Wright's thinking, for he next places against those first impressions the image of an isolated particular, in this case a lone gull:

> . . . high in a cloud, a single naked gull
> Shadows a depth in heaven for the eye.

And the ear, the other organ of sensory perception indispensable to poetry, learns an order of sound from the chaos of received sensations:

> And, for the ear, under the wail and snarl
> Of groping foghorns and the winds grown old,
> A single human word for love of air
> Gathers the tangled discords up to song.

In subsequent lines a statement of aesthetics of a sort not strange to readers of contemporary literature is offered. This notion of the poem is based on a belief in rigorous economy of expression, the exact relationship of part to part, and part to whole; it demands as well, "the rare word for the rare desire." Wright holds to his dominant sea imagery, demonstrating his aesthetic outlook as he presents it; the gull is changed into his metaphor for the poem:

> Summon the rare word for the rare desire.
> It thrives on hunger, and it rises strong
> To live above the blindness and the noise
> Only as long as bones are clean and spare,
> The spine exactly set, the muscles lean.
> Before you let a single word escape,

Starve it in darkness; lash it to the shape
Of tense wing skimming on the sea alone . . .

From here on the poem moves in a direction somewhat
different from the one it has taken thus far. The poet confesses that the "careful rules of song" he had certainly
expected to compose and deliver to a friend (Gerald
Enscoe, to whom the poem is addressed) with a "cold
lucidity of heart" have not been completed, for he has
been caught up and distracted by the ceaseless animation
of the seascape. He seems to be saying that his ideas
about poetry—its sources and craft, its connections with
reality—must be modified in the face of reality. The
moon rises, altering the scene and "flaunting to nothingness the rules" he intended to set forth. Reality now
assumes the upper hand; it is not something the poet can
simply shape to his own will and personal measurement
but a dimension of things he must enter, to whose being
he must submit himself ("Where the sea moves, the word
moves, where the sea/ Subsides, the slow word fades with
lunar tides"). What he gives to his friend at the conclusion are "echoes of [his] voice" that apparently partake
of the sea, the moon, and the restless interplay of elements that have so absorbed him. His poem, we guess,
will be a poem of the reality that goes into its making;
thus it will fulfill Whitman's wish by learning its essential patterns and laws from reality.

As he did in *The Green Wall*, Wright in *Saint Judas*
devotes poems to persons whose lives have brought them
to the far side of society's moral boundaries. "American
Twilights," "At the Executed Murderer's Grave," and
"Saint Judas" are outstanding demonstrations of this
poet's obsession with themes of guilt and innocence,
justice and punishment, moral right and hypocrisy. Furthermore, these poems show a distinct advance to a
franker, more straightforward manner, which is linked,
in turn, to the very evident involvement of the poet as

an individual in the experience conveyed by the poem. Wright outspokenly blends his voice with that of Jesus' betrayer in the dramatic monologue of "Saint Judas." While this device might not seem any more intimate than is usual with our poet, we perceive quite suddenly that the radical twist he gives to the narrative and the tragic force of its conclusion are distinctively his own:

> When I went out to kill myself, I caught
> A pack of hoodlums beating up a man.
> Running to spare his suffering, I forgot
> My name, my number, how my day began,
> How soldiers milled around the garden stone
> And sang amusing songs; how all that day
> Their javelins measured crowds; how I alone
> Bargained the proper coins, and slipped away.
>
> Banished from heaven, I found this victim beaten,
> Stripped, kneed, and left to cry. Dropping my
>   rope
> Aside, I ran, ignored the uniforms:
> Then I remembered bread my flesh had eaten,
> The kiss that ate my flesh. Flayed without hope,
> I held the man for nothing in my arms.

From this sonnet we can understand, easily enough, Wright's strong feelings about the ambiguities of human motive and behavior, the differences—in the story of Judas as told here—between design and impulse. Because man is at one moment weak and treacherous, and at another moment brave and selfless, it is implied that he should be more sparing in the judgment of his fellows and freer with his mercy.

"At the Executed Murderer's Grave" strengthens our awareness of the invisible bonds existing between people, outcasts and criminals included. In this poem Wright puts himself at the center, engaged in the activity of meditation. The poem begins with his self-declaration, but it goes on to consider the figure of George Doty, executed Ohio murderer, whose life and guilt are finally seen as unavoidably entangled with the poet's, for when "the princes of the sea come down/ To lay away their robes, to judge the earth/ And its dead" he, James Wright (and the rest of us with him), will have our "sneaking crimes" revealed too. The tone is matter-of-fact, but sharp; the lines, though rhyming, are blunt, at times rhythmically choppy. A quality of undiluted directness prevails throughout the poem. The last stanza serves as a climax to the poet's thoughts about the dead man and to the harsh self-examination they have provoked:

> Doty, the rapist and the murderer,
> Sleeps in a ditch of fire, and cannot hear;
> And where, in earth or hell's unholy peace,
> Men's suicides will stop, God knows, not I.
> Angels and pebbles mock me under trees.
> Earth is a door I cannot even face.
> Order be damned, I do not want to die,
> Even to keep Belaire, Ohio, safe.
> The hackles on my neck are fear, not grief.
> (Open, dungeon! Open, roof of the ground!)
> I hear the last sea in the Ohio grass,
> Heaving a tide of gray disastrousness.
> Wrinkles of winter ditch the rotted face
> Of Doty, killer, imbecile, and thief:
> Dirt of my flesh, defeated, underground.

The emphasis on a mood close to dreamlike subjectivity which gradually replaces argument and logical thought in the stanza above prepares the way into James Wright's most recent poetry. That poetry is still regional in the sense previously mentioned; and I think it would not be misleading to call certain poems pastoral, for they do adopt the Minnesota countryside and farmlands as the setting for a calm, reflective—if not perfectly idyllic —mode of living. Shepherds may be missing, but animals are not; Wright has created a haunting yet delicate poem about the kinship between men and horses in "A Blessing":

Just off the highway to Rochester, Minnesota,
Twilight bounds softly forth on the grass.
And the eyes of those two Indian ponies
Darken with kindness.
They have come gladly out of the willows
To welcome my friend and me.
We step over the barbed wire into the pasture
Where they have been grazing all day, alone.
They ripple tensely, they can hardly contain their
        happiness
That we have come.
They bow shyly as wet swans. They love each
        other.
There is no loneliness like theirs.
At home once more,
They begin munching the young tufts of spring in
        the darkness.
I would like to hold the slenderer one in my arms,
For she has walked over to me
And nuzzled my left hand.
She is black and white,
Her mane falls wild on her forehead,
And the light breeze moves me to caress her long
        ear
That is delicate as the skin over a girl's wrist.
Suddenly I realize
That if I stepped out of my body I would break
Into blossom.

This lovely poem from Wright's third collection, *The Branch Will Not Break* (1963), makes plain, as do the other poems in the book, his very decisive innovations in style, in concern and approach. In the first place, the music and rhythm of these new poems is noticeably

different; as Lowell does so often in *Life Studies*, and
Roethke in some of his later work, Wright employs extremely free lines of irregular length and yet never loses
his rhythmical coherence. This change helps to account
for the gentle, thoughtful quality, the relaxed character
so prominent in "A Blessing." But there is a second
change that is perhaps more important, a change in the
kind and arrangement of imagery. Wright is not alone
in his new poetic practices. Robert Bly, with whom
Wright has been in close association in the past few
years, is a solid and vocal proponent of these changes
too, both in his own poetry (*Silence in the Snowy Fields*,
1962) and in the critical pieces he has written for the
journal he edits, *The Sixties*, and for John Logan's peri-
odical of poetry, *Choice*. Another poet who has lately
given proof of similar interests is Louis Simpson (*At the
End of the Open Road*, 1963), though he lives in California, half way across the country from the Minnesota
residents Bly and Wright. Wright has not, to my knowledge, put down in print any of his ideas about his recent
writing, except to say that "from now on [it] will be entirely different"; and so we must rely on Bly's prose for
a little guidance. It should be trustworthy guidance, however, because his poems and Wright's are so obviously
allied in spirit. In the introductory paragraphs of an om-
nibus poetry review published in *Choice, 2*, Bly discusses
the element of "inwardness" which, he feels, distin-
guishes the true modern poem and is so scarce in the
English and American verse of our time:

> Poetry, by breaking up the stanza and moving to-
> ward inwardness, is creating for itself a way of ex-
> pression open to new thought. It is creating for itself
> an instrument of knowledge, a poem, responsive en-
> tirely to the imagination. Poetry's purpose in grow-
> ing is to advance deeper into the unknown country
> . . . . In order to penetrate into this country poetry

must learn to sleep differently, to awake differently, to listen for new sounds, to walk differently.

What is the unknown country? It is a change in inward life which corresponds to the recent changes in outward life. Let us consider some of the changes in outward life in the last hundred years: colonialism dies, engines are born, the religions lose power, business takes power. The change has been thorough. The change penetrates deeper than we believe. Poetry has been able to describe this inward change better than fiction has. Neruda tells us more about modern life than Faulkner; Rilke tells us more than Mann.

All around us are huge reservoirs of bypassed emotions, ignored feelings, unexplained thoughts. As Rilke said to sculptors, there are hundreds of gestures being made which we are not aware of. The purpose of poetry is to awaken the half of us that has been asleep for many years—to express thoughts not yet thought. All expression of hidden feelings involves opposition to the existing order. Among the great poets of this century who sense this meaning of poetry most strongly Rainer Maria Rilke of Germany, Pablo Neruda of Chile, and Cesar Vallejo of Peru stand out. But there are strong American poets also.

Unfortunately, we are not told who these American poets are, for Bly proceeds to his business at hand in this essay, which is the review of a number of new books of verse. I do not wish to attribute all of Bly's ideas to James Wright, but I think we cannot avoid the fact that in practice both poets attempt to create a poetry of the type described above. Such a poetry relies to a considerable degree on sources below the level of consciousness or of rational thought ("thoughts not yet thought"). Of course, most poetry has always depended upon these wellsprings in the preconscious and the unconscious, but the question raised here is really aimed at the disposition of this material for poetic ends. Reading the recent poetry of Wright, Simpson, Bly, Merwin, and also some of the poems of James Dickey, such as "The Owl King" and "Drowning with Others," one notices how frequently they mold their work around a group of images deriving from subliminal regions of the mind and joined by associations of an emotional, symbolic, and lyrical kind. We must not mistake this enterprise for the automatic writing and revolutionary philosophy of the French Surrealists, even though Bly speaks of "hidden feelings" at odds with "the existing order" in a manner slightly reminiscent of André Breton. To begin with, we cannot for an instant doubt the intervention and exercise of conscious craftsmanship upon the imagery of poems such as Wright's, a violation of Surrealism's iron-clad laws of irrationality without interference. We might indicate, too, that not all of the images used by these poets are dredged from the subconscious. Second, I believe that the sort of opposition to the existing state of things advocated by Bly, while it may involve politics, is directed primarily toward a renewal of sensibilities, a more comprehensive vision of the world.

What we do find very often in the poems of Wright or Bly is a fluid, dreamlike construction; each poem seems to mirror a condition of intense subjectivity, a moment of extreme perception personal to the poet and yet capable of stirring subtle and profound responses in the reader. Donald Hall adds something more to this point in the introduction to *Contemporary American Poetry*. The writers we have been discussing, Hall maintains, have put to work "a new kind of imagination" in their poetry. "This new imagination reveals through images a subjective life which is *general*, and which corresponds to an old objective life of shared experience and knowledge." Hall's italicized word *general* aids us further in understanding the appeal of Wright's or Bly's or Simpson's imagery, for that imagery circumvents the rational intelligence to strike far into the interior world of emotions and memories, there to awaken forgotten portions of the affective life.

In the poem "Fear Is What Quickens Me," Wright investigates through the web he fashions of irrational but carefully woven images themes of human guilt and anxiety growing out of the ties between man and other creatures, the conquest and urbanization of America (really the urbanization of the modern world), and man's own divided and frustrated nature. The poem is arranged in three sections of sharply diminishing size, but increasing force:

1

Many animals that our fathers killed in America
Had quick eyes.
They stared about wildly,
When the moon went dark.
The new moon falls into the freight yards
Of cities in the south,
But the loss of the moon to the dark hands of
    Chicago
Does not matter to the deer
In this northern field.

2

What is that tall woman doing
There, in the trees?
I can hear rabbits and mourning doves whispering
    together
In the dark grass, there
Under the trees.

3

I look about wildly.

Logical explication of such a poem will not be easy, nor will it necessarily be to the point. The poet appears to discourage that conventional approach by the very way he writes. An alternative is an absorbing of the poem which will permit its images, their suggestiveness, to permeate the reader's mind gradually.

In telling us how poems of inwardness voice their opposition to the status quo, Bly implies, among other things, a love for the rural mode of existence which both he and James Wright juxtapose with the urban environment augmented by our contemporary technological and industrial gains. The two settings are plain in the city images and in the pastoral qualities and meditative lyricism of *The Branch Will Not Break*. Moral passion, which generated an ample part of Wright's earlier writing, has been assimilated by the new poetic method. His criticisms now submit themselves to the ruling influence of the imagery rather than depend upon any declared moral purpose. The total effect of this imagery is slow and cumulative; it is in accord with the actual movement of the poems, with their free but apt rhythms, their shifting but calculated emphases.

Wright's later kind of political and moral criticism, in the poem "Eisenhower's Visit to Franco, 1959", for example, embodies the same lyrical and imagistic material we have in the less topical pieces, but here the magnificently evocative imagery is tinged with irony. To make his position perfectly clear, Wright draws into the middle of this poem about state and military leaders and their powerful troops the lone figure of one of the greatest twentieth-century Spanish poets, Antonio Machado, and through him recalls not only the negative theme of exile but, more affirmatively, the perennial life of Spain, unchanged by Franco's dictatorship. The last stanza, however, again stresses the leaders of state and their force of arms. Wright's critical attitude upholds the ancient human patterns of Spain against the encroaching pres-

sures of the abstract, impersonal state that bosses like
Franco try to impose upon the country and its inhabitants.
The poem's epigraph is borrowed from the Spanish philosopher and poet Miguel de Unamuno: ". . . we die
of cold, and not of darkness."

The American hero must triumph over
The forces of darkness.
He has flown through the very light of heaven
And come down in the slow dusk
Of Spain.

Franco stands in a shining circle of police.
His arms open in welcome.
He promises all dark things
Will be hunted down.

State police yawn in the prisons.
Antonio Machado follows the moon
Down a road of white dust,
To a cave of silent children
Under the Pyrenees.
Wine darkens in stone jars in villages.
Wine sleeps in the mouths of old men, it is a dark
    red color.

Smiles glitter in Madrid.
Eisenhower has touched hands with Franco,
    embracing
In a glare of photographers.
Clean new bombers from America muffle their
    engines
And glide down now.
Their wings shine in the searchlights
Of bare fields,
In Spain.

Personal perceptions begin many of Wright's new poems, as they did previous ones. In their own fashion Wright, Bly, Simpson, and Merwin are as autobiographical as the more explicitly confessional poets, Robert Lowell, Anne Sexton, W. D. Snodgrass, and Galway Kinnell. We are constantly aware of a particular active consciousness in Wright's work, a consciousness that sometimes dwells on its own history and that generally makes its presence felt as the single agent of what we see and know in any poem. Thus there are poems definitely inaugurated by moments in their author's life; "Having Lost My Sons . . . ," "Milkweed," "Mary Bly," "A Blessing," "I Was Afraid of Dying," "Lying in a Hammock at William Duffy's Farm . . . ," and "A Dream of Burial" are among the finest of them. But even these pieces, their specific details picked from Wright's living experience, from events in his biography, assume, through the poetic means by which they are incarnated, the aspect of dream or of trancelike vision that is peculiar to *The Branch Will Not Break.* In "A Dream of Burial" the poet foresees his own death, the slow-motion (so true to the quality of dreams) of his dismemberment, and the period of waiting the soul must be subjected to before beginning its last journey to a final resting-place. Though the dream belongs to Wright's personal experience, it is doubtless a shared dream, including as it does archetypal images of imagined death in the whitened bones, the mausoleum building, the chorus of mourners, the corridor which is another place of burial but also the way of exodus for the soul, the sea as symbol of eternity or God, and the horse as vehicle for the journeying spirit:

> Nothing was left of me
> But my right foot
> And my left shoulder.
> They lay white as the skein of a spider floating
> In a field of snow toward a dark building

Tilted and stained by wind.
Inside the dream, I dreamed on.

A parade of old women
Sang softly above me,
Faint mosquitos near still water.

So I waited, in my corridor.
I listened for the sea
To call me.
I knew that, somewhere outside, the horse
Stood saddled, browsing in grass,
Waiting for me.

Poetry of this sort links James Wright to Roethke, Eberhart, and Kunitz in their visionary and mystical moods. Yet Wright's later technique, which he has partially in common with Bly and Simpson, has no parallel in the writing of his predecessors in America with the exception of Roethke, whose sequence poems of psychic life in *The Lost Son* and *Praise to the End* are similar in their scheme of juxtaposing images from the preconscious mind. Yet one has to look elsewhere for the poets who have inspired Wright most thoroughly. Some of them are named in the passage quoted from Robert Bly—Rilke, Neruda, Vallejo—but there are others, Trakl, Jimenez, Machado, Lorca, and Chinese poets among them. Both Wright and Bly have published translations from many of these writers, and their appearance is fresh and different and stimulating for American literature. It would be a serious mistake, though, to explain away Wright's newest poetry through his reading. In less than a decade he has reached the forefront of contemporary poets and by his own accomplishments he has advanced our imaginative frontiers.

XII

Anne Sexton

Anne Sexton is, by any standards, a bold and impressive poet. At first glance, the unsuspecting reader may be jolted by the self-revelation that so plainly serves as the basic raw material of her art. To be sure, we have already discussed personal disclosure as it is variously employed in the writing of Robert Lowell, Brother Antoninus, Denise Levertov, and James Wright; but few poets—perhaps Lowell and Antoninus are the chief exceptions—have attempted to convey the feeling of the continuity of a single life, the poet's own, in something approximating its full complexity. Undisguised revelation and examination—of her parents, her lovers, her friends; of the unbelievable torment of both mental and physical illness as she has had to endure them; of her struggles with a religious belief that eludes her but doesn't leave her; of the face of death as she has frequently seen it—comprise Mrs. Sexton's poetic cosmos. The eye the poet brings to bear on these contents of her life is mercilessly lucid; yet she can be compassionate toward others and is without self-pity. Her life, as must be clear by now, has been graced only slightly with what we ordinarily conceive as happiness; its occasional joys and moments of tenderness are wrung from the general pain of experience. Yet these pleasures and affections are the more precious because of the cost involved in obtaining them, and also because of the poet's strong love which brings them about in spite of the odds. Mrs. Sexton has further discovered an ability to introduce order into existence, to allow valued things to survive through the imaginative act that in the making of a poem can create its own patterns of justice, meaning, and love. Lacking a firm religious faith, she seeks in the performance of her work a redeeming task:

> My friend, my friend, I was born
> doing reference work in sin, and born
> confessing it. This is what poems are:
> with mercy
> for the greedy,
> they are the tongue's wrangle,
> the world's pottage, the rat's star.
>   ("With Mercy for the Greedy")

In her first book, *To Bedlam and Part Way Back* (1960), Anne Sexton concentrates her sharp and fertile imagination a number of times on the period of her mental illness and hospitalization, as well as on the effects of this illness in her relationships with others (her daughter and mother, for instance, in "The Double Image"). One of the best poems directly treating the subject, "Ringing the Bells," should help to demonstrate, through its frighteningly realistic picture of therapy at a hospital, the kind of marvelous artistic proficiency combined with an uncompromising vision of human actuality that we can usually expect of Mrs. Sexton. The mixture of simplicity and sophistication in rhythm and diction, building up through one long sentence, terrible in its understatement, and concluding in another, three-word sentence that compresses all the agony and helplessness and resignation of her dilemma, exhibits this

poet's brilliant technical mastery, in addition to her
toughness of mind, to real advantage:

> And this is the way they ring
> the bells in Bedlam
> and this is the bell-lady
> who comes each Tuesday morning
> to give us a music lesson
> and because the attendants make you go
> and because we mind by instinct,
> like bees caught in the wrong hive,
> we are the circle of the crazy ladies
> who sit in the lounge of the mental house
> and smile at the smiling woman
> who passes us each a bell,
> who points at my hand
> that holds the bell, E flat,
> and this is the grey dress next to me
> who grumbles as if it were special
> to be old, to be old,
> and this is the small hunched squirrel girl
> on the other side of me
> who picks at the hairs over her lip,
> who picks at the hairs over her lip all day,
> and this is how the bells really sound,
> as untroubled and clean
> as a workable kitchen,
> and this is always my bell responding
> to my hand that responds to the lady
> who points at me, E flat;
> and although we are no better for it,
> they tell you to go. And you do.

A few poems, such as "You, Doctor Martin" and "Said
the Poet to the Analyst," present different, and less har-
rowing, accounts of her days of hospitalization and psy-
chiatric treatment. Still other poems like "Music Swims
Back to Me" and "Her Kind" undertake to render the au-

thor's disturbed psychic and spiritual states; certain less directly focused poems like "The Double Image" and "Lullaby" occasionally touch this theme. This spell of confinement and the poems dealing with it provide merely one part of the life Mrs. Sexton suggests to us. She sometimes includes poems that do not depend upon her biography but are efforts to step into more objective dramatic or lyrical roles; but these pieces are, in my opinion, generally weaker because so much of this poet's power lies in her talent for dramatizing *her own* existence in the wide range of its moods, memories, relationships, aspirations, desires, and for doing this without evading the necessary consequence of having to face herself squarely in the mirror of her art.

Mrs. Sexton also devotes poems in this first book to her parents and other close relatives, a practice that carries over into her next collection. She traces with the utmost scrupulousness her own attitudes in these family relations. What we get, in a phrase borrowed from the title of a poem about the poet, her daughter, and her mother, is a type of "double image," in which the subject of the particular poem and, simultaneously, the poet's ties with and approach to that subject are sketched. Through this indirect but revelatory method we learn even more about the poet herself.

The predominant mood of the family poems is elegiac. Mrs. Sexton's parents are both dead—her mother died of cancer, her father died a few months after her mother; her brother was killed on a beachhead during the war; the great aunt she loved so fiercely in her childhood succumbed to deafness and to a resulting mental breakdown. Thus the poetry founded on such figures is one of bittersweet memory and loss. The elegy for her brother, "For Johnny Pole on the Forgotten Beach," admirably exhibits these qualities. The poem starts out with a fairly long stanza of pleasant recollections of summers on the beach as children. There they rode the breakers in, sunned themselves, and dreamed their futures. The boy's last name even becomes evocative of youth, stalwartness, and masculine potentiality as the poet describes him:

> In his tenth July some instinct
> taught him to arm the waiting wave,
> a giant where its mouth hung open.
> He rode on the lip that buoyed him there
> and buckled him under. The beach was strung
> with children paddling their ages in,
> under the glare of noon chipping
> its light out. He stood up, anonymous
> and straight among them, between
> their sand pails and nursery crafts.
> The breakers cartwheeled in and over
> to puddle their toes and test their perfect
> skin. He was my brother, my small
> Johnny brother, almost ten. We flopped
> down upon a towel to grind the sand
> under us and watched the Atlantic sea
> move fire, like night sparklers;
> and lost our weight in the festival
> season. He dreamed, he said, to be
> a man designed like a balanced wave . . .
> how someday he would wait, giant
> and straight.
>
> Johnny, your dream moves summers
> inside my mind.

Following the brief transition in the last lines above, the poem leaps across another decade in the poet's memory. The scene of the second long stanza is again a beach, but this one Mrs. Sexton has had to imagine for herself in all its horror and waste. At its edge is sprawled the dead body of her brother, aged twenty. With an overwhelming yet deft irony she introduces words and images recalling the happy innocence and human possibility of the earlier stanza into the depiction of its tragic outcome. The beach, the youthful bodies with their connotation of life's copious physical vitality, the waves, the bright, warm sunlight of another ocean, and the posture of the brother are warped out of recognition—or perhaps we should say that they are still recognizable enough to thrust their terrible implication upon us:

> He was tall and twenty that July,
> but there was no balance to help;
> only the shells came straight and even.
> This was the first beach of assault;
> the odor of death hung in the air
> like rotting potatoes; the junkyard
> of landing craft waited open and rusting.
> The bodies were strung out as if they were
> still reaching for each other, where they lay
> to blacken, to burst through their perfect
> skin. And Johnny Pole was one of them.
> He gave in like a small wave, a sudden
> hole in his belly and the years all gone
> where the Pacific ocean chipped its light out.
> Like a bean bag, outflung, head loose
> and anonymous, he lay. Did the sea move fire
> for its battle season? Does he lie there
> forever, where his rifle waits, giant
> and straight? . . . I think you die again
> and live again,
>
> Johnny, each summer that moves inside
> my mind.

In poem after poem Mrs. Sexton discloses to us her mind populated and haunted, as it is in this elegy for her brother, by persons and events of the past, reviving them in the act of writing and so bringing to them through her imagination the mutual effort of love and understanding. That is true of the pair of poems about her mother with which her initial book finishes, and likewise fits several pieces in *All My Pretty Ones* (1962) about her father and her family life when she was a girl. Another early poem, "Some Foreign Letters," develops a very moving description of the poet's great aunt from a group of letters she left behind. In Paul Engle's and Joseph Langland's anthology *Poet's Choice*, Mrs. Sexton has made some observations about this poem:

> "Some Foreign Letters" is a mixture of truth and lies. I don't feel like confessing which is which. When I wrote it I attempted to make all of it "true." It remains true *for me* to this day. But I will say that it was written to my great aunt who came to live with us when I was about nine and very lonely. She stayed with us until she had a nervous breakdown. This was triggered by her sudden deafness. I was seventeen at the time she was taken away. She was, during the years she lived with us, my confidante and my comforter. I never thought of her as being young. She was an extension of myself and my world. I hadn't considered that she might have had a world of her own once. Many years later, after her death, I found a bound volume of her letters from Europe. (My family were the type that bound letters in leather.) The letters are gay and intimate and tragic.

As the poem begins Mrs. Sexton sits perusing the dead aunt's letters and, at the same time, remembering the aunt as she knew her in old age. The world this aunt so freely traveled and the experiences she recorded in her correspondence come to the poet out of a "graceful innocent age," one the latter "loved," as she notes in *Poet's Choice*, "but never knew." The opening stanza then goes on to offer a summary picture based on the letters that captures beautifully and succinctly the flavor of life for

this New England woman journeying through Europe
at the end of the nineteenth century. We need also to
see how Mrs. Sexton keeps us conscious both of her presence as a reader of the letters and as the person who
recalls a later phase of the aunt's life and so can contrast
it with the earlier.

> You posted them first in London, wearing furs
> and a new dress in the winter of eighteen-ninety.
> I read how London is dull on Lord Mayor's Day,
> where you guided past groups of robbers, the sad
>   holes
> of Whitechapel, clutching your pocketbook, on
>   the way
> to Jack the Ripper dissecting his famous bones.
> This Wednesday in Berlin, you say, you will
> go to a bazaar at Bismarck's house. And I
> see you as a young girl in a good world still,
> writing three generations before mine. I try
> to reach into your page and breathe it back . . .
> but life is a trick, life is a kitten in a sack.

The final line of this stanza predicts the fate awaiting
the young lady traveler, first in disappointments, ultimately in her sudden attack of deafness and nervous collapse. Indications of Johnny Pole's destiny are not so
obvious in the first half of the poem about him. The
trick of fate is nearly a commonplace in Mrs. Sexton's
work, as apparently it has been in her experience. The
"kitten in a sack," one of this poet's most unbalancing
metaphors, points to human helplessness in the grip of
forces that unexpectedly twist individual lives from their
normal course, threaten them, or lead them to conclusion without warning. We are all, the implication runs,
included in the image of that kitten imprisoned in a sack
and will be drowned at last. However, any translation of
the line's significance pales next to the line itself; Mrs.
Sexton uses her metaphor to great effect. As she muses

on her aunt's letters the past and future (though both
of these are now periods of the past from the writer's
location in time) fall together, with a death in between:
the beloved aunt has escaped "the sack of time" and left
the poet to bind the pieces of her life for her.

The poem continues, and further excerpts from the
aunt's European travels turn up, occasionally interrupted
by the poet's memories of the dissolution of what that
lady had known and been:

> This is Italy. You learn its mother tongue.
> I read how you walked on the Palatine among
> the ruins of the palaces of the Caesars;
> alone in the Roman autumn, alone since July.
> When you were mine they wrapped you out of
>   here
> with your best hat over your face. I cried
> because I was seventeen. I am older now.

In the last years of her life she had come to stay with
Mrs. Sexton's parents, as the remarks from *Poet's Choice*
explain. The aunt's world, the world of the 1880s, as the
poet sees, had long since crumbled into an unfamiliar and
disastrous age. This old lady's expectations, the most important ones, have gone unfulfilled. Her romance with
a German count was fruitless. She finishes as a spinster
great-aunt loved by a young girl who, much later, will
discover her letters and start to comprehend her life. In
the closing stanza Mrs. Sexton summons with dexterity
and deeply felt emotion the pathos of a person's existence whose hopes have dispersed and whose conclusion
is near. In spite of the inevitable human failure, the
poet's love and sympathy reinforce the aunt's persistent
endeavor to speak her own truth, and lend this last stanza
a sense of redemption:

> Tonight I will learn to love you twice;
> learn your first days, your mid-Victorian face.
> Tonight I will speak up and interrupt

your letters, warning you that wars are coming,
that the Count will die, that you will accept
your America back to live like a prim thing
on the farm in Maine. I tell you, you will come
here, to the suburbs of Boston, to see the blue-nose
world go drunk each night, to see the handsome
children jitterbug, to feel your left ear close
one Friday at Symphony. And I tell you,
you will tip your boot feet out of that hall,
rocking from its sour sound, out onto
the crowded street, letting your spectacles fall
and your hair net tangle as you stop passers-by
to mumble your guilty love while your ears die.

Redemption, as was previously suggested, arrives by
the poem, so far as Mrs. Sexton is concerned. In her
poetry character, motive, and experience receive evalua-
tion and judgment; in this respect she is one of those
poets who seems to be winning back property that fiction
writers had almost completely annexed. And, of course,
Mrs. Sexton is presenting a segment of her own life when
she portrays her aunt or some other person, for that life
is the true origin of her poetry.

Anne Sexton's new poems, gathered in *All My Pretty
Ones* (the title of which, taken from *Macbeth*, suggests
a preoccupation with death and ruin), though they sacrifice none of their harsh devotion to the facts of experience, do enter some different areas of her life as well as
resuming prior explorations. Several notable poems are
given over to her family relationships when she was a
girl; her father is portrayed, as her mother was in the
preceding book. In "The Truth the Dead Know," an
elegy for both parents, she leaves the place of their death
and burial in an attempt to regain, by geographical
change and the play of the senses, her awareness of being alive:

We drive to the Cape. I cultivate
myself where the sun gutters from the sky,
where the sea swings in like an iron gate
and we touch. In another country people die.

Nature seems barely to agree with human wishes in these
lines: the guttering sun, the mechanical motion of
the sea are, at best, indifferent; at worst, sinister. Human
contact does, however, provide momentary relief before
the final stanza puts us back where we began with the
disquieting question, "And what of the dead?" That
stanza ends with the poet's realization of her small com-
forts of the flesh that her mother and father, by dying,
have relinquished: "They refuse/to be blessed, throat,
eye and knucklebone."

The truth the dead know in the poem of that title
contributes an integral part of the knowledge with which
Mrs. Sexton tries to meet her experience. Such recognition of mortality colors the whole of her vision, even
though she is still quite capable of salvaging images of
beauty from the prospect of general destruction. The
life of the body and the temporary warmth of love it
can feel are always endangered by the exacting costs of
time or by disorder and loss. Again, in the somewhat
longer poem "The Operation," the poet takes as a point
of departure the grim coincidence that she too is suspected of having cancer just a short while after her
mother's death from the disease. Once she submits to
the indignities of the doctor's examination, the precari-
ousness of existence has become a fundamental theme:

After the sweet promise,
the summer's mild retreat
from mother's cancer, the winter months of her
    death,
I come to this white office, its sterile sheet,
its hard tablet, its stirrups, to hold my breath
while I, who must, allow the glove its oily rape,

to hear the almost mighty doctor over me equate
my ills with hers
and decide to operate.

The next stanzas look retrospectively over her mother's
Ilness and the last months of her life. At the opening
»f the second section we are confronted with the poet
)repared for surgery, her body deprived of its identity:
he hangs suspended, a floating consciousness in a flesh
;one alien, between memories of past pleasure and a fu-
ure in which she has no certainty of existing. Waiting
Ills her mind with nightmares of tense expectancy:

> Clean of the body's hair,
> I lie smooth from breast to leg.
> All that was special, all that was rare
> is common here. Fact: death too is in the egg.
> Fact: the body is dumb, the body is meat.
> And tomorrow the O.R. Only summer was sweet.
>
> The rooms down the hall are calling
> all night long, while the night outside
> sucks at the trees. I hear limbs falling
> and see yellow eyes flick in the rain. Wide eyed
> and still whole I turn in my bin like a shorn lamb.
> A nurse's flashlight blinds me to see who I am.

In these stanzas Mrs. Sexton apprehends within the
human individual the seeds of his own decay and death.
Like Dylan Thomas, who saw the conclusion of life con-
tained in the instant of its conception, she thinks of herself in sacrificial terms, as "a shorn lamb." (A comparison
of this sacrificial theme of surgery might profitably be
made with W. D. Snodgrass' poem "The Operation.")
And the operation realizes her premonitions as she passes
into a bizarre universe where the spirit, lacking any control, must live out the victimized body's fate. The course
pursued by her mind or spirit in an anaesthetic dream

draws near to death, but then returns; the poet's self cut and patched, is reborn to a world almost lost:

> The great green people stand
> over me; I roll on the table
> under a terrible sun, following their command
> to curl, head touching knee if I am able.
> Next, I am hung up like a saddle and they begin.
> Pale as an angel I float out over my own skin.
>
> I soar in hostile air
> over the pure women in labor,
> over the crowning heads of babies being born.
> I plunge down the backstair
> calling *mother* at the dying door,
> to rush back to my own skin, tied where it was
>   torn.
> Its nerves pull like wires
> snapping from the leg to the rib.
> Strangers, their faces rolling like hoops, require
> my arm. I am lifted into my aluminum crib.

The poem closes with its author, her "stomach laced up like a football/for a game," getting ready to take up ordinary living again. But that resumption does not put an end to Mrs. Sexton's thought, nor does it resolve the problems to which she is heir. Given her acute sensitivity to human frailty, to the agonies built in men's bones which she knows so well and has stated so plentifully in her verse, we could guess that she must finally grapple with questions of supernatural belief. Indeed, in *To Bedlam and Part Way Back* the last poem, "The Division of Parts," entertains a comparison between the poet's sorting of goods her mother has willed her and the dividing of Christ's possessions after His crucifixion. The religious parallel is called up naturally because Mrs. Sexton notices that the day on which she is performing her difficult family duty is Good Friday. Her meditations

prompt her to consider both her religious upbringing and
her present state of skepticism:

> The clutter of worship
> that you taught me, Mary Gray,
> is old. I imitate
> a memory of belief
> that I do not own. I trip
> on your death and Jesus, *my stranger*
> floats up over
> my Christian home, wearing his straight
> thorn tree. I have cast my lot
> and am one third thief
> of you. Time, that rearranger
> of estates, equips
> me with your garments, but not with grief.

Mrs. Sexton's concern with faith extends to *All My
Pretty Ones*, specifically to a series of poems grouped in
one section of that book and prefaced by the following
statement of the Catholic theologian Romano Guardini:
"I want no pallid humanitarianism—if Christ be not
God, I want none of him; I will hack my way through
existence alone. . . ."

We cannot take it for granted that these words, written by a man of profound religious faith, automatically
assert Mrs. Sexton's belief, when they would appear in
fact to signify her selection of the alternative: stoicism,
loneliness, and self-reliance. But if this is her choice, it
has not been lightly made, as the poems of this group
indicate. Three that strike at the very heart of Mrs. Sexton's interests involve the figure of Christ: "With Mercy
for the Greedy," "For God While Sleeping," and "In
the Deep Museum." Since she is a poet without mystical
inclinations, but rather is earthbound, committed to a
vision that shocks by its unvarnished realism, it is hardly
surprising that she should approach religious belief
through the person of Christ, who is, for her, the man

claiming to be God and subjecting Himself to the ex
tremes of bodily and spiritual torture as proof of Hi
appointed task. He is the one who reminds her again c
the destiny to which all flesh is ordered—death. Th
Christ she envisages so vividly recalls the beaten, ravage
images of the Crucifixion painted by Gruenewald and
in our own time, by Graham Sutherland. The poem "Fo
God While Sleeping" displays the durable human emo
tion she feels for Christ. It first mentions the poet's ow
sickness, but shifts in revery to Jesus' sufferings. The
brutal details should not be permitted to obscure Mrs
Sexton's compassion and the desire she has to resolve
her troubled relationship with this crucified figure who
inhabits her dreams:

> Sleeping in fever, I am unfit
> to know just who you are:
> hung up like a pig on exhibit,
> the delicate wrists,
> the beard drooling blood and vinegar;
> hooked to your own weight,
> jolting toward death under your nameplate.
>
> Everyone in this crowd needs a bath.
> I am dressed in rags.
> The mother wears blue. You grind your teeth
> and with each new breath
> your jaws gape and your diaper sags.
> I am not to blame
> for all this. I do not know your name.
>
> Skinny man, you are somebody's fault.
> You ride on dark poles—
> a wooden bird that a trader built
> for some fool who felt
> that he could make the flight. Now you roll
>   in your sleep, seasick
> on your own breathing, poor old convict.

There is a development from the first hallucinatory
mages growing out of the poet's fitful sleep in the begin-
ing stanza to a participation in the milling crowd wit-
essing the Crucifixion; then, after further comment on
Christ which seems adverse but is really tender, the dream
ubsides. "Poor old convict" is not very clear and may
uggest several meanings, the most likely of which is, I
hink, an identification of the poet's fate with that of
Christ—that is, the conclusion of all human effort in fail-
ire and death. This identification is, of course, based on
he premise that Christ's execution is an example of de-
eat for an idealist ("some fool who felt/that he could
nake the flight"), and so Mrs. Sexton's own skepticism
emains unchanged. But these last lines are perhaps too
onfused, too much like a dream, for us to be certain of
dentities. In any case, the suffering caused by the poet's
llness, her feverish condition, allows the vision to form
nd links her in feeling to the dying Christ. The next
oem, "In the Deep Museum," retains the device of fan-
asy and nightmare speculation in order to articulate the
houghts of Jesus, who, having been crucified, awakens
n the sepulchre only to die a more horrible and degrad-
ng death, a death that succeeds (if that is the poet's
im) in turning the idea of the Resurrection into a
ideous mockery.

Mrs. Sexton's poetry, then, is built upon an attitude of
toic pessimism that occasionally lapses into morbidity;
et we cannot doubt the biting honesty of her intelligence or the truth *to her* of the intuitions around which
her art is modeled. There is also a more delightful side
o some of her work; this is particularly evident in the
xuberant lyricism of "Letter Written on a Ferry While
Crossing Long Island Sound." In this poem she imagines
hat four nuns who are fellow-passengers on the ferry
vithout warning "rise out/over this greasy deck" and
ascend into the sky above the open waters. Here are two
tanzas that give the general atmosphere:

Dearest,
see how my dark girls sally forth,
over the passing lighthouse of Plum Gut,
its shell as rusty
as a camp dish,
as fragile as a pagoda
on a stone;
out over the little lighthouse
that warns me of drowning winds
that rub over its blind bottom
and its blue cover;
winds that will take the toes
and the ears of the rider
or the lover.

There go my dark girls,
their dresses puff
in the leeward air.
Oh, they are lighter than flying dogs
or the breath of dolphins;
each mouth opens gratefully,
wider than a milk cup.
My dark girls sing for this.
They are going up.

The poems Anne Sexton has published so far read like
the pages of an autobiography in verse which expose her
without defense, though this is true only if we accept for
a moment that poetry *is* her mode of defense and self
comprehension. It is precisely this fact which saves her
work from the weaknesses of exhibitionism or of vain
subjectivity. The private experience that Mrs. Sexton
holds up so courageously to frank, imaginative scrutiny
falls outside her possession once the poem has been
written: that experience is transformed into a public one,
that is to say, one capable of illuminating the lives of
each of us.

Epilogue

Poetry is a lonely occupation. That is perhaps the first lesson learned in examining literary practice from Hölderlin or Blake or Baudelaire—wherever one likes to assign a somewhat arbitrary beginning for modern poetry—to the American poets studied in the preceding chapters. Undoubtedly, loneliness always has been one of the poet's occupational hazards; at the moment of composition, the poet is necessarily alone, whether he happens to be in a crowded restaurant or by himself in his room. But there is a further experience of spiritual isolation which the modern poet knows deep in his bones, an isolation generated and maintained by his continuing rejection of the aims and ideologies of society, and by its neglect of his work and the vision of life presented there. As a result, the poet is in the curious but fruitful (in terms of his art) position of repudiating, or at least sharply criticizing, directly or indirectly, the institutions, the religion and morality, the accepted ideals, the veneration of technology and material goods, the inhuman wars, and the fundamental hypocrisy that comprise our society from a vantage point within that society. Indeed, his basic desire is not to flee society but in some sense to be its independent, living conscience, for if the contemporary poet is more of a dreamer than the man in the street, he is far less of an escapist.

It is precisely this position, of what we might call an alienated inhabitant, that belongs to our twelve poets and to most of their contemporaries. The perspective their location affords is not easily come by because it combines the two activities of participation and objectification—of experiencing the life of our time and making of that experience poetry—and so it involves more than mere dissatisfaction with the world of urban living and hydrogen bombs. In fact, we should say that this perspective is won only through the life of the imagination, which integrates the knowledge derived from experience with the formal demands of art. In the poet's case, the life of the imagination is directed toward the truth of self and reality as it can be discovered concretely through the means of language and its music; this truth is trusted over any delivered through abstractions or by the impersonal dictation of authority.

Thus the main requirements of the poetic endeavor as we have been observing it in this book (and here, of course, I am assuming in advance the gifts and skills of craftsmanship) are absolute integrity and an openness to the full human experience; either without the other would create a disequilibrium that would throw the imagination off balance. Are not integrity and openness prime attributes of our twelve poets? Do we not see the capacity for retaining a singularity of mind and, simultaneously, for permitting the elements of reality, the life of the world as it is encountered, to resound in the depths of the self? Richard Eberhart makes of his consciousness a testing ground for opposing types of insight and attempts to transcend them; in Theodore Roethke's poems we find the evolution of the self relived in all its terror and joy, until, finally, the self penetrates to the heart of creation; Karl Shapiro, Stanley Kunitz, and James Wright take upon themselves the burdens of pain, suffering, and guilt, the spiritual and physical torments inflicted on men by their fellows in our century; for Elizabeth Bishop, Richard Wilbur, Isabella Gardner, and Denise Levertov the ordinary objects and events, the trivial details of actuality, are worthy of the closest attention, and, once known in their marvelous particularity, arouse a feeling of spiritual exultation and discovery; the poems of Brother Antoninus, Robert Lowell, and Anne Sexton dispense with masks and fictional disguises to reveal the significance of their authors' experience as it was lived.

Each of these poets has, then, exposed himself to the conditions of existence as it has been presented, and has ordered it according to a certain vision. This confrontation of and vulnerability to actuality (the "participation" that precedes "objectification," to recall my earlier terms) leads to the understanding and compassion from which the poets' moral responses spring. Those responses, if we can risk generalizing about them and momentarily separate them from the poetry which is their embodiment, honor the individual and the particular over against the mass or the hypothetical or the dogmatic. So we have noticed the contemporary poet championing the social or moral outcast (James Wright in "Sappho," and Stanley Kunitz in "The Surgeons"), bitterly attacking the inhuman techniques of modern warfare (Richard Eberhart in "The Fury of Aerial Bombardment"), or harshly deriding legacies of pride and bigotry that still threaten us (Robert Lowell in "The First Sunday in Lent" and Karl Shapiro in "University"). Identifying himself with the solitary individual, with the life of the person in its distinctness, the poet there takes his moral stance. And though he frequently dismisses religion in its organized, institutional forms as too nearly allied with the prevailing interests and opinions of society, his sympathy for the individual and his sufferings, his indignation at human folly and injustice, his sense of the mystery surrounding birth and death and man's spiritual being, his reverence for the creatures and things and the seasonal rhythms of the natural world, his intense belief in the value of the communion of selves, and of love (sexual or otherwise), make of his art a kind of unofficial religious statement— heterodox perhaps but firmly rooted in the values of the Judaeo-Christian tradition. The poet can provide in some ways a much more vital and accurate conscience than dogma or pronouncement, for his work is a concrete instance of experience and, therefore, is closer to the complexities of our existence. But this is said without intending, as Matthew Arnold, I. A. Richards, or Wallace Stevens (each in his own fashion) would have it, that poetry should be a *substitute* for religion.

Beyond the moral concerns mentioned, there is a religious intuition which brings to some poets moments of heightened visionary or mystical perception. We have seen this intuition active in the writings of Richard Eberhart and Theodore Roethke especially, and to a lesser degree in recent poems by James Wright and Denise Levertov. It is worth remarking, I think, in support of my emphasis on the *specific* and *personal* aspects of the contemporary poets' explorations, that none of them attempts to enlarge these perceptions into a system or to fit them into any particular theological or speculative framework of ideas. We may interpret this refusal as the indication of a common reluctance to attach poems to anything outside themselves and their own immediate, sensuous grasp of experience.

Poetry is, then, the lonely occupation we spoke of, but that is only half the story. Poetry is viewed by the poet as an essential spiritual task in which meaning and value are conferred upon the raw matter of experience through its imaginative transformation. The previous chapters have attempted to illustrate the different ways in which contemporary poets undertake this task by meeting the reality that lies to hand, the reality within the radius of their actual lives. Every day, it seems, the modern world grows more impersonal, more mechanical and abstract, more threatening, and the circumference or range of personal life appears to shrink correspondingly. However ominous this tendency may be, it has returned the poet to certain fundamentals, for he can at least speak authentically of his own sphere of knowledge and perception, can evaluate through his art things and acts in *his* existence, can chart the *personal space* he inhabits as a physical and spiritual being. Contemporary poets have, as we noted previously, forsaken many of the grand symbolic gestures of their predecessors—the mythologies of Yeats or Rilke, the eclectic historicism of Pound—replacing them with the intensity of the individual, personal voice speaking to us through every facet of the poem, and, in addition, speaking to us from the core of an experience that begins as the poet's but achieves its total significance only as readers share in it as a work of art. Kenneth Rexroth's sentences on this relationship from his *Bird in the Bush: Obvious Essays* (1959) make a fitting conclusion to our discussions and bring us to the reading of the poetry itself:

The arts presume to speak directly from person to person, each polarity, the person at each end of the communication fully realized. The speech of poetry is from me to you, transfigured by the overcoming of all thingness—reification—in the relationship. So speech approaches in poetry not only the directness and the impact but the unlimited potential of act. . . . The work of art has about it an immediacy of experience of the sort that many people never manage in their daily lives. At the same time it has an illimitable character. Speech between you and me is focused, but spreads off indefinitely and immeasurably. What is communicated is self to self—whole "universes of discourse."

Bibliography

WORKS BY RICHARD EBERHART:

A Bravery of Earth. New York, Jonathan Cape & Harrison Smith, 1930.

Reading the Spirit. New York, Oxford University Press, 1937.

Song and Idea. New York, Oxford University Press, 1942.

Poems, New and Selected. Norfolk, Conn., New Directions, 1944.

Burr Oaks. New York, Oxford University Press, 1947.

Selected Poems. New York, Oxford University Press, 1951.

Undercliff: Poems 1946-1953. New York, Oxford University Press, 1953.

Great Praises. New York, Oxford University Press, 1957.

Collected Poems 1930-1960. New York, Oxford University Press, 1960.

Collected Verse Plays. Chapel Hill, University of North Carolina Press, 1962.

The Quarry: New Poems. New York, Oxford University Press, 1964.

WORKS BY STANLEY KUNITZ:

Intellectual Things. Garden City, N. Y., Doubleday, 1930.

Passport to the War. New York, Henry Holt, 1944.

Selected Poems 1928-1958. Boston and Toronto, Atlantic: Little, Brown, 1958.

WORKS BY THEODORE ROETHKE:

Open House. New York, Knopf, 1941.

The Lost Son and Other Poems. Garden City, N. Y., Doubleday, 1948.

Praise to the End! Garden City, N. Y., Doubleday, 1951.

The Waking: Poems 1933-1953. Garden City, N. Y., Doubleday, 1953.

Words for the Wind. Garden City, N. Y., Doubleday, 1958.

I Am! Says the Lamb. Garden City, N. Y., Doubleday, 1961.

Sequence, Sometimes Metaphysical. Iowa City, Stone Wall Press, 1964.

The Far Field. Garden City, N. Y., Doubleday, 1964.

On the Poet and His Craft: Selected Prose of Theodore Roethke, Ralph J. Mills, Jr., ed. Seattle, University of Washington Press, 1965.

WORKS BY ELIZABETH BISHOP:

North and South. Boston, Houghton Mifflin, 1946.

Poems: North and South & A Cold Spring. Boston, Houghton Mifflin, 1955.

WORKS BY BROTHER ANTONINUS (WILLIAM EVERSON):

(William Everson) *These Are the Ravens.* San Leandro, Calif., Pamphlet Series of Western Poets, 1935.

(William Everson) *The Masculine Dead.* Iowa City, James Decker, 1942.

(William Everson) *The Residual Years.* New York, New Directions, 1948.

The Crooked Lines of God. Detroit, University of Detroit Press, 1959.

The Hazards of Holiness. Garden City, N. Y., Doubleday, 1962.

WORKS BY KARL SHAPIRO:

Person, Place and Thing. New York, Reynal & Hitchcock, 1942.

V-Letter. New York, Reynal & Hitchcock, 1944.

Essay on Rime. New York, Reynal & Hitchcock, 1945.

Trial of a Poet. New York, Reynal & Hitchcock, 1947.

Poems 1940-1953. New York, Random House, 1953.

Beyond Criticism. Lincoln, University of Nebraska Press, 1953.

Poems of a Jew. New York, Random House, 1958.

In Defense of Ignorance. New York, Random House, 1960.

The Bourgeois Poet. New York, Random House, 1964.

WORKS BY ISABELLA GARDNER:

Birthdays from the Ocean. Boston, Houghton Mifflin, 1955.

The Looking Glass. Chicago, University of Chicago Press, 1961.

WORKS BY ROBERT LOWELL:

Land of Unlikeness. Cummington, Mass., The Cummington
　　Press, 1944.

Lord Weary's Castle. New York, Harcourt, Brace, 1946.

The Mills of the Kavanaughs. New York, Harcourt, Brace,
　　1951.

Life Studies. New York, Farrar, Straus & Cudahy, 1959.

Imitations. New York, Farrar, Straus & Cudahy, 1961.

For the Union Dead. New York, Farrar, Straus & Giroux,
　　1964.

WORKS BY RICHARD WILBUR:

The Beautiful Changes and Other Poems. New York, Reynal
　　& Hitchcock, 1947.

Ceremony and Other Poems. New York, Harcourt, Brace,
　　1950.

Molière's The Misanthrope. New York, Harcourt, Brace,
　　1955.

Things of This World. New York, Harcourt, Brace, 1956.

Candide: A Comic Opera (with Lillian Hellman and others).
　　New York, Random House, 1957.

Advice to a Prophet and Other Poems. New York, Harcourt,
　　Brace, 1961.

The Poems of Richard Wilbur. New York, Harcourt, Brace
　　& World, 1963.

WORKS BY DENISE LEVERTOV:

The Double Image. London, Cresset Press, 1946.

Here and Now. San Francisco, City Lights Books, 1957.

Overland to the Islands. Highlands, N. C., Jonathan Wil-
　　liams, 1958.

With Eyes at the Back of Our Heads. New York, New Di-
　　rections, 1959.

The Jacob's Ladder. New York, New Directions, 1961.

O Taste and See. New York, New Directions, 1964.

WORKS BY JAMES WRIGHT:

The Green Wall. New Haven, Conn., Yale University Press,
　　1957.

Saint Judas. Middletown, Conn., Wesleyan University Press,
　　1959.

The Branch Will Not Break. Middletown, Conn., Wesleyan
　　University Press, 1963.

WORKS BY ANNE SEXTON:

To Bedlam and Part Way Back. Boston, Houghton Mifflin, 1960.

All My Pretty Ones. Boston, Houghton Mifflin, 1962.

CRITICISM:

Allen, Don Cameron, ed., *The Moment of Poetry*. Baltimore, Johns Hopkins Press, 1962.

> Papers by John Holmes, May Sarton, Richard Eberhart, Richard Wilbur, and Randall Jarrell on poetry in general and on specific works.

The American Scholar, 28:3 (Summer, 1959).

> A special issue on contemporary American poetry with essays by Randall Jarrell, Donald Hall, Robert Langbaum, and A. Alvarez.

Cambon, Glauco, *Recent American Poetry*. Minneapolis, University of Minnesota Press, 1962.

> A useful monograph which treats in detail some younger poets, starting with Wilbur and including Galway Kinnell, John Logan, W. S. Merwin, and others. Also contains a helpful bibliography.

Deutsch, Babette, *Poetry in Our Time*. Garden City, N. Y., Anchor Books: Doubleday, 1963.

> A lengthy but excellent study of modern poetry and poets with a number of comments on contemporary Americans.

Eckman, Frederick, *Cobras and Cockle Shells: Modes in Recent Poetry*. The Sparrow Magazine, Vagrom Chapbook Number Five, 1958.

> An interesting discussion of a variety of poetic techniques in the work of younger writers.

Hungerford, Edward B., ed., *Poets in Progress: Critical Prefaces to Ten Contemporary Americans*. Evanston, Ill., Northwestern University Press, 1962.

> Studies by ten critics of Roethke, Lowell, Kunitz, Wilbur, Eberhart, Snodgrass, Nemerov, Cunningham, Jarrell, Merwin.

Jarrell, Randall, *Poetry and the Age*. New York, Vintage Books: Knopf, 1955.

> Although it is not devoted to poetry of the contemporary period alone, this collection of essays has been

enormously influential in various ways since its appearance.

Kizer, Carolyn, "Poetry of the Fifties: in America," in John Wain, ed., *International Literary Annual I* (New York, 1959), pp. 60-96.
A valuable survey of veteran poets and newcomers.

Kunitz, Stanley, "Poetry's Silver Age: An Improbable Dialogue," in John Fischer and Robert B. Silvers, eds., *Writing in America* (New Jersey, 1960), pp. 27-45.
A statement of the character and diversity of present-day American verse.

Nemerov, Howard, *Poetry and Fiction: Essays.* New Brunswick, N. J., Rutgers University Press, 1963.
This poet's collected essays include a number of perceptive reviews of his juniors and his contemporaries.

Ossman, David, *The Sullen Art.* New York, Corinth Books: Citadel Press, 1963.
Radio interviews with Rexroth, Carroll, Blackburn, Rothenberg, Kelly, Bly, Logan, Sorrentino, Creeley, Merwin, Levertov, Jones, Dorn, Ginsberg.

Ostroff, Anthony, ed., *The Contemporary Poet as Artist and Critic.* Boston, Little, Brown, 1964. Eight symposia on poems by Eberhart, Roethke, Kunitz, Lowell, Wilbur, Ransom, Auden, and Shapiro with replies by these poets. All participants are themselves distinguished poets. A very valuable book.

Ransom, John Crowe, Schwartz, Delmore, and Wheelock, John Hall, *American Poetry at Mid-Century.* Washington, D.C., Library of Congress, 1958.
Three lectures on problems of recent poetry.

Rosenthal, M. L., *The Modern Poets: A Critical Introduction.* New York, Oxford University Press, 1960.
A thorough and perceptive study of modern poetry that concentrates on established figures such as Eliot, Yeats, and Pound but also discusses a good many later poets.

Shapiro, Karl, *Essay on Rime.* New York, Reynal and Hitchcock, 1945.
A critical essay in verse on matters of prosody, language, and belief.

ANTHOLOGIES AND COLLECTIONS:

Allen, Donald M., *The New American Poetry 1945-1960*. New York, Grove Press, 1960.

> A large anthology of poets representative of interests and tendencies not often given official critical sanction; includes Ashbery, Antoninus, Carroll, Creeley, Corso, Duncan, Ginsberg, O'Hara, Snyder, and Williams. It provides bibliographies and "Statements on Poetics" by a number of the contributors.

Big Table, I:4, 1960.

> A special issue devoted to "The New American Poets" that contains work by Blackburn, Logan, Creeley, Carroll, Ginsberg, Ashbery, Snyder, and others, and several prose pieces on these poets and their methods.

Bosquet, Alain, ed., *Trente-cinq Jeunes Poètes Américains*. Paris, Gallimard, 1960.

> A wide selection of contemporary verse ranging from Roethke and Shapiro to Ashbery and Ferlinghetti. The editor's preface offers a different perspective on American poetic attitudes and practices.

Ciardi, John, ed., *Mid-Century American Poets*. New York, Twayne, 1950.

> An important and valuable collection of poems by Wilbur, Viereck, Rukeyser, Roethke, Shapiro, Scott, Nims, Mayo, Lowell, Jarrell, Holmes, Eberhart, Ciardi, Bishop, and Schwartz with prefatory comments by the poets.

Elliott, George P., ed., *Fifteen Modern American Poets*. New York, Rinehart, 1956.

> Ample selections, with a preface and helpful notes, from the work of Bishop, Eberhart, Jarrell, Lowell, Miles, Nemerov, Plutzik, Roethke, Rukeyser, Schevill, Schwartz, Scott, Shapiro, Warren, and Wilbur.

Engle, Paul, and Langland, Joseph, eds., *Poet's Choice*. New York, Dial Press, 1962.

> More than one hundred English, Irish, Canadian, and American poets select a favorite poem from their own work and comment on the choice.

Hall, Donald, ed., *Contemporary American Poetry*. Baltimore, Penguin Books, 1963.

An excellent representative collection of recent American poetry containing work by Stafford, Lowell, Duncan, Whittemore, Nemerov, Wilbur, Dickey, Hecht, Levertov, Logan, Simpson, Bowers, Justice, Bly, Creeley, Merrill, Snodgrass, Ashbery, Kinnell, Merwin, Wright, Kennedy, Rich, Snyder, and Mezey, and a fine introduction.

Hall, Donald, Pack, Robert, and Simpson, Louis, eds., *The New Poets of England and America*. New York, Meridian Books: World, 1957.

An extensive anthology of poems by writers "under forty" at the time of publication.

Hall, Donald, and Pack, Robert, eds., *The New Poets of England and America: Second Selection*. Cleveland and New York, Meridian Books: World, 1962.

Some of the same poets as in the First Selection but all new work; also an introduction to the English poets by Hall, to the Americans by Pack.

Stern, Richard G., ed., "American Poetry of the Fifties," *The Western Review*, 21:3 (Spring 1957).

A special issue with a preface by Stern and poetry by, among others, Belvin, Bowers, Carroll, Gardner, Justice, Merrill, Merwin, Pack, Rich, Snodgrass, Simpson, Stafford, Swenson, Woods, and Wright.

OTHER POETS AND THEIR WORK
(*Some Suggested Further Readings*):

Ammons, A. R., *Expressions of Sea Level*. Columbus, Ohio State University Press, 1963.

Ashbery, John, *Some Trees*. New Haven, Conn., Yale University Press, 1956.

The Tennis Court Oath. Middletown, Conn., Wesleyan University Press, 1963.

Baro, Gene, *Northwind*. New York, Scribners, *Poets of Today* VI, 1959.

Belitt, Ben, *Wilderness Stair*. New York, Grove Press, 1955.

The Enemy Joy. Chicago, University of Chicago Press, 1964.

Berryman, John, *The Dispossessed*. New York, William Sloane: Morrow, 1948.

> *Homage to Mistress Bradstreet*. New York, Farrar, Straus, 1956.

> *77 Dream Songs*. New York, Farrar, Straus, 1964.

Blackburn, Paul, *The Dissolving Fabric*. Highlands, N. C., Divers Press, 1955.

Bly, Robert, *Silence in the Snowy Fields*. Middletown, Conn., Wesleyan University Press, 1962.

Bowers, Edgar, *The Form of Loss*. Denver, Alan Swallow, 1956.

Boyle, Kay, *Collected Poems*. New York, Knopf, 1962.

Brinnin, John Malcolm, *Selected Poems*. Boston, Atlantic: Little, Brown, 1963.

Brooks, Gwendolyn, *Selected Poems*. New York and Evanston, Harper and Row, 1963.

Burden, Jean, *Naked as the Glass*. New York, Clarke and Way, 1963.

Burford, William, *A World*. Austin, University of Texas Press, 1962.

Carrier, Constance, *The Middle Voice*. Denver, Alan Swallow, 1955.

Carruth, Hayden, *The Crow and the Heart*. New York, Macmillan, 1959.

> *Journey to a Known Place*. New York, New Directions, 1961.

> *The Norfolk Poems*. Iowa City, Prairie Press, 1962.

Ciardi, John, *As If*. New Brunswick, N. J., Rutgers University Press, 1955.

> *I Marry You*. New Brunswick, N. J., Rutgers University Press, 1958.

> *39 Poems*. New Brunswick, N. J., Rutgers University Press, 1959.

> *In the Stoneworks*. New Brunswick, N. J., Rutgers University Press, 1961.

> *In Fact*. New Brunswick, N. J., Rutgers University Press, 1962.

Corso, Gregory, *Gasoline*. San Francisco, City Lights Bookshop, 1958.

    Happy Birthday of Death. New York, New Directions, 1960.

Coxe, Louis O., *The Sea-Faring*. New York, Holt, 1947.

    The Second Man. Minneapolis, University of Minnesota Press, 1955.

    The Wilderness. Minneapolis, University of Minnesota Press, 1958.

    The Middle Passage. Chicago, University of Chicago Press, 1960.

Creeley, Robert, *For Love: Poems 1950-1960*. New York, Scribners, 1962.

Dickey, James, *Into the Stone*. New York, Scribners, *Poets of Today* VII, 1960.

    Drowning with Others. Middletown, Conn., Wesleyan University Press, 1962.

    Helmets. Middletown, Conn., Wesleyan University Press, 1963.

Dickey, William, *Of the Festivity*. New Haven, Conn., Yale University Press, 1959.

    Interpreter's House. Columbus, Ohio State University Press, 1963.

Dorn, Edward, *The Newly-Fallen*. New York, Totem Press, 1961.

Dugan, Alan, *Poems*. New Haven, Conn., Yale University Press, 1961.

    Poems 2. New Haven, Conn., Yale University Press, 1963.

Duncan, Robert, *Selected Poems*. San Francisco, City Lights Bookshop, 1959.

    Letters. Highlands, N. C., Jonathan Williams, 1958.

    The Opening of the Field. New York, Grove Press, 1960.

    Roots and Branches. New York, Scribners, 1964.

Eigner, Larry, *On My Eyes*. Highlands, N. C., Jonathan Williams, 1960.

English, Maurice, *Midnight in the Century*. Park Forest, Ill., Prairie School Press, 1964.

Evans, Abbie Huston, *Fact of Crystal*. New York, Harcourt, Brace and World, 1961.

Fearing, Kenneth, *New and Selected Poems*. Bloomington, Indiana University Press, 1956.

Feldman, Irving, *Works and Days*. Boston, Atlantic: Little, Brown, 1961.

Ferlinghetti, Lawrence, *Pictures of the Gone World*. San Francisco, City Lights Bookshop, 1955.

    A Coney Island of the Mind. New York, New Directions, 1957.

    Starting from San Francisco. New York, New Directions, 1961.

Fitzgerald, Robert, *In the Rose of Time: Poems 1931-1956*. New York, New Directions, 1956.

Francis, Robert, *The Orb Weaver*. Middletown, Conn., Wesleyan University Press, 1960.

Garrigue, Jean, *The Ego and the Centaur*. New York, New Directions, 1947.

    The Monument Rose. New York, Noonday Press; Farrar, Straus and Cudahy, 1953.

    A Water Walk by Villa d'Este. New York, Macmillan, 1959.

    Country Without Maps. New York, Macmillan, 1964.

Gibbs, Barbara, *The Green Chapel*. New York, Noonday Press; Farrar, Straus and Cudahy, 1958.

Ginsberg, Allen, *Howl*. San Francisco, City Lights Bookshop, 1956.

    Kaddish. San Francisco, City Lights Bookshop, 1961.

Gregory, Horace, *Collected Poems*. New York, Holt, Rinehart and Winston, 1964.

Guest, Barbara, *Poems*. Garden City, N.Y., Doubleday, 1962.

Guthrie, Ramon, *Graffiti*. New York, Macmillan, 1959.

Hall, Donald, *Exiles and Marriages*. New York, Viking Press, 1955.

    Dark Houses. New York, Viking Press, 1958.

    A Roof of Tiger Lilies. New York, Viking, 1964.

Hayden, Robert, *Ballad of Remembrance*. London, Paul Bremen, 1962.

Hecht, Anthony, *A Summoning of Stones*. New York, Macmillan, 1954.

The Seven Deadly Sins. Northampton, Mass., Gehenna Press, 1958.

Hirschman, Jack, *A Correspondence of Americans*. Bloomington, Indiana University Press, 1960.

Hoffman, Daniel, *An Armada of Thirty Whales*. New Haven, Conn., Yale University Press, 1954.

A Little Geste. New York, Oxford University Press, 1960.

The City of Satisfactions. New York, Oxford University Press, 1963.

Hollander, John, *A Crackling of Thorns*. New Haven, Conn., Yale University Press, 1958.

Movie-Going. New York, Atheneum, 1962.

Holmes, John, *Address to the Living*. New York, Twayne, 1937.

The Double Root. New York, Twayne, 1950.

The Fortune Teller. New York, Harper, 1961.

Howes, Barbara, *In the Cold Country*. New York, Bonacio and Saul: Grove Press, 1954.

Light and Dark. Middletown, Conn., Wesleyan University Press, 1959.

Humphries, Rolfe, *Poems: Collected and New*. New York, Scribners, 1954.

Ignatow, David, *The Gentle Weightlifter*. New York, Morris Gallery, 1955.

Say Pardon. Middletown, Conn., Wesleyan University Press, 1961.

Figures of the Human. Middletown, Conn., Wesleyan University Press, 1964.

Jarrell, Randall, *Selected Poems*. New York, Knopf, 1955.

The Woman at the Washington Zoo. New York, Atheneum, 1960.

The Lost World. New York, Atheneum, 1965.

Jones, LeRoi, *Preface to a Twenty Volume Suicide Note*. New York, Totem Press, 1960.

Justice, Donald, *The Summer Anniversaries*. Middletown, Conn., Wesleyan University Press, 1960.

A Local Storm. Iowa City, Stone Wall Press, 1963.

Kees, Weldon, *Collected Poems*. Lincoln, University of Nebraska Press, 1962.

Kennedy, X. J., *Nude Descending a Staircase*. New York, Doubleday, 1961.

Kessler, Milton, *A Road Came Once*. Columbus, Ohio State University Press, 1963.

Kinnell, Galway, *What a Kingdom It Was*. Boston, Houghton Mifflin, 1960.
  Flower Herding on Mount Monadnock. Boston, Houghton Mifflin, 1964.

Kizer, Carolyn, *The Ungrateful Garden*. Bloomington, Indiana University Press, 1961.

Koch, Kenneth, *Ko, or A Season on Earth*. New York, Grove Press, 1959.
  Thank You. New York, Grove Press, 1962.

Laing, Dilys, *Walk Through Two Landscapes*. New York, Twayne, 1949.
  Poems from a Cage. New York, Macmillan, 1961.

Lang, V. R., *The Pitch: Poems and Plays*. New York, privately printed, 1962.

Langland, Joseph, *The Green Town*. New York, Scribners, *Poets of Today III*, 1956.
  The Wheel of Summer. New York, Dial Press, 1963.

Lattimore, Richmond, *Poems*. Ann Arbor, University of Michigan Press, 1957.
  Sestina for a Far-Off Summer. Ann Arbor, University of Michigan Press, 1962.

Laughlin, James, *Selected Poems*. New York, New Directions, 1959.

Logan, John, *Cycle for Mother Cabrini*. New York, Grove Press, 1955.
  Ghosts of the Heart. Chicago, University of Chicago Press, 1960.
  Spring of the Thief. New York, Knopf, 1963.

Meredith, William, *Love Letter from an Impossible Land*. New Haven, Conn., Yale University Press, 1944.
  Ships and Other Figures. Princeton, Princeton University Press, 1948.
  The Open Sea. New York, Knopf, 1957.
  The Wreck of the Thresher. New York, Knopf, 1964.

Merrill, James, *First Poems*. New York, Knopf, 1951.

      Country of a Thousand Years of Peace. New York, Knopf, 1959.

      Water Street. New York, Atheneum, 1962.

Merton, Thomas, *Selected Poems*. New York, New Directions, 1959.

      Emblems of a Season of Fury. New York, New Directions, 1963.

Merwin, W. S., *A Mask for Janus*. New Haven, Conn., Yale University Press, 1952.

      The Dancing Bears. New Haven, Yale University Press, 1954.

      Green with Beasts. London, Rupert Hart-Davis, 1956.

      The Drunk in the Furnace. New York, Macmillan, 1960.

      The Moving Target. New York, Atheneum, 1963.

Mezey, Robert, *The Lovemaker*. Iowa City, Cummington Press, 1961.

Miles, Josephine, *Poems 1930-1960*. Bloomington, Indiana University Press, 1960.

Miller, Vassar, *Wage War on Silence*. Middletown, Conn., Wesleyan University Press, 1960.

      My Bones Being Wiser. Middletown, Conn., Wesleyan University Press, 1963.

Moss, Howard, *A Winter Come, A Summer Gone: Poems 1946-1960*. New York, Scribners, 1960.

Nemerov, Howard, *The Image and the Law*. New York, Holt, 1947.

      Guide to the Ruins. New York, Random House, 1950.

      The Salt Garden. Boston, Little, Brown, 1955.

      Mirrors and Windows. Chicago, University of Chicago Press, 1958.

      New and Selected Poems. Chicago, University of Chicago Press, 1960.

      The Next Room of the Dream. Chicago, University of Chicago Press, 1963.

Nims, John Frederick, *The Iron Pastoral*. New York, William Sloane, 1947.

      A Fountain in Kentucky. New York, William Sloane, 1950.

Knowledge of the Evening. New Brunswick, N.J., Rutgers University Press, 1960.

O'Gorman, Ned, *The Night of the Hammer*. New York, Harcourt, Brace, 1959.

Adam Before His Mirror. New York, Harcourt, Brace, 1961.

The Buzzard and the Peacock. New York, Harcourt, Brace, 1964.

O'Hara, Frank, *Meditations in an Emergency*. New York, Grove Press, 1957.

Second Avenue. New York, Totem Press, 1960.

Olson, Charles, *The Maximus Poems*. New York, Jargon: Corinth Books, 1960.

The Distances. New York, Grove Press, 1960.

Olson, Elder, *Collected Poems*. Chicago, University of Chicago Press, 1963.

Oppen, George, *The Materials*. New York, New Directions, 1962.

Pack, Robert, *The Irony of Joy*. New York, Scribners, *Poets of Today II*, 1955.

A Stranger's Privilege. New York, Macmillan, 1959.

Guarded by Women. New York, Random House, 1963.

Patchen, Kenneth, *Selected Poems*. New York, New Directions, 1957.

Plath, Sylvia, *The Colossus*. New York, Knopf, 1962.

Plutzik, Hyam, *Apples from Shinar*. Middletown, Conn., Wesleyan University Press, 1959.

Horatio. New York, Atheneum, 1961.

Rago, Henry, *A Sky of Late Summer*. New York, Macmillan, 1963.

Rexroth, Kenneth, *The Phoenix and the Tortoise*. New York, New Directions, 1944.

The Signature of All Things. New York, New Directions, 1949.

In Defense of the Earth. New York, New Directions, 1956.

Natural Numbers: New and Selected Poems. New York, New Directions, 1963.

Reznikoff, Charles, *By the Waters of Manhattan*. New York, New Directions, 1962.

Rich, Adrienne Cecile, *A Change of World*. New Haven, Conn., Yale University Press, 1951.
The Diamond Cutters. New York, Harper, 1955.
Snapshots of a Daughter-in-Law. New York, Harper and Row, 1963.

Rukeyser, Muriel, *Waterlily Fire: Poems 1935-1962*. New York, Macmillan, 1962.

Sarton, May, *Cloud, Stone, Sun, Vine: Poems Selected and New*. New York, Norton, 1961.

Schubert, David, *Initial A*. New York, Macmillan, 1961.

Schwartz, Delmore, *Summer Knowledge: New and Selected Poems 1938-1958*. Garden City, N.Y., Doubleday, 1959.

Scott, Winfield Townley, *Collected Poems 1937-1962*. New York, Macmillan, 1962.

Simpson, Louis, *The Arrivistes*. New York, Fine Editions Press, 1950.
Good News of Death. New York, Scribners, *Poets of Today II*, 1955.
A Dream of Governors. Middletown, Conn., Wesleyan University Press, 1959.
At the End of the Open Road. Middletown, Conn., Wesleyan University Press, 1963.

Smith, William Jay, *Poems 1947-1957*. Boston, Atlantic: Little, Brown, 1957.

Snodgrass, W. D., *Heart's Needle*. New York, Knopf, 1959.

Snyder, Gary, *Rip-Rap*. Ashland, Mass., Origin Press, 1959.
Myths and Texts. New York, Totem Press, 1960.

Sorrentino, Gilbert, *The Darkness Surrounds Us*. Highlands, N.C., Jonathan Williams, 1960.

Stafford, William, *West of Your City*. Los Altos, Calif., Talisman Press, 1960.
Travelling Through the Dark. New York and Evanston, Harper and Row, 1962.

Sward, Robert, *Kissing the Dancer*. Ithaca, N. Y., Cornell University Press, 1964.

Swenson, May, *To Mix with Time: New and Selected Poems*. New York, Scribners, 1963.

Viereck, Peter, *Terror and Decorum*. New York, Scribners, 1948.

    Through the Mask. New York, Scribners, 1950.

    The First Morning. New York, Scribners, 1952.

    The Persimmon Tree. New York, Scribners, 1956.

    The Tree Witch. New York, Scribners, 1961.

Wagoner, David, *Dry Sun, Dry Wind*. Bloomington, Indiana University Press, 1953.

    A Place to Stand. Bloomington, Indiana University Press, 1958.

    The Nesting Ground. Bloomington, Indiana University Press, 1963.

Weiss, Theodore, *Outlanders*. New York, Macmillan, 1960.

    Gunsight. New York, New York University Press, 1962.

Whittemore, Reed, *An American Takes a Walk*. Minneapolis, University of Minnesota Press, 1956.

    The Self-Made Man. New York, Macmillan, 1959.

    The Boy from Iowa. New York, Macmillan, 1962.

    The Fascination of the Abomination. New York, Macmillan, 1963.

Williams, Jonathan, *The Empire Finals at Verona*. Highlands, N.C., Jonathan Williams, 1959.

    Amen, Huzza, Selah. Highlands, N.C., Jonathan Williams, 1960.

    In England's Green &. San Francisco, Auerhahn Press, 1962.

    Lines About Hills Above Lakes. Fort Lauderdale, Fla., Roman Books, 1964.

Zaturenska, Marya, *Selected Poems*. New York, Grove Press, 1954.

    Terraces of Light. New York, Grove Press, 1960.

Index